Constructing a Successful Children's Ministry

A Christian Teaching Tool

1. It doesn't matter if you have five kids or fifty kids, you can minister to them on a weekly basis by using simple techniques taught in this handbook.

2. Do you need Sunday School teachers or nursery workers? We answer questions on how to train new teachers—and how to keep the ones you have so that they won't experience 'burn out'!

3. Do you want your children involved? Encourage them to do puppets, dance, choir, and drama to prepare them for ministry as an adult.

4. Do you need a training tool? You can use this handbook to create workshops for your own ministry.

Constructing a Successful Children's Ministry

A Christian Teaching Tool

SHARON WICKER
AND REBECCA COOK

Constructing a Successful Children's Ministry

A Christian Teaching Tool

Sharon Wicker and Rebecca Cook

Published August 2014
Little Creek Books
Imprint of Jan-Carol Publishing, Inc
All rights reserved
Copyright © 2014 by Sharon Wicker and Rebecca Cook
Front Cover Illustration: Amanda Rasnake
Book Design: Tara Sizemore

In keeping within the copyright ownership, this book may be reproduced only in part as a teaching tool and instructional guide and may not be reproduced as a commercial product for selling purposes. Written special requests granted only by written permission to avoid infringement.

ISBN: 978-1-939289-48-3
Library of Congress Control Number: 2014949298

You may contact the publisher:
Jan-Carol Publishing, Inc
PO Box 701
Johnson City, TN 37605
E-mail: publisher@jancarolpublishing.com
Website: jancarolpublishing.com

To everyone who has worked in children's ministry, may God bless you—
for every child you lead to Christ;
for every seed you have planted in their hearts;
for every prayer you say,
including boo-boo prayers, pet prayers, and salvation prayers;
and for your faithfulness to study, prepare, teach—
and then clean up—week after week,
We commend you!

Dear Reader

We have been asked so many times the questions on every children's pastor's mind: "*How do we keep workers? How do we train teachers? How should we discipline children?*" After searching the scriptures and doing our best to answer these tough questions, we were compelled to share our insights.

As children's pastors ourselves, we have served nursery-schoolers through 12-year-olds for many years. We have learned many valuable teaching strategies to make our weekly classes flow more smoothly, and we have trained teachers for their roles. We have spoken at many children's conferences. In all of these settings, we have experienced both incredible frustration and huge waves of success.

After preparing innumerable handouts, sermons, and presentations, we realized that we should compile all of this time and information into a handbook. So we poured everything we have taught, learned, and experienced into this wonderful tool. We pray that this handbook is an asset for any size church, for any denomination, and for anyone involved in children's ministry, from novice teachers to experienced directors and pastors.

Blessings on you and your ministry,
Sharon and Rebecca

Table of Contents

Acknowledgements — ix
Imparting a Vision for Children's Ministry — x

Part I: Foundations of Children's Ministry

Is There Not a Cause for a Biblically Sound Children's Ministry? — 1
Why Teach Children? — 8
How to Begin a Children's Ministry — 10
Planning for Success — 16
Recruiting Staff — 19
Organizing for Growth — 22
The Teacher's Image — 25
Encouraging Students to Be Their Best — 28
Planning and Organizing Big Events — 33
Promotion of Big Events — 37
Sample Itemized Director's List for Large Events — 40
Class Promotion — 42
The Responsibilities of a Children's Pastor — 46
Coordinator Responsibilities — 52

Part II: Ministry in the Classroom

Ice Breakers–Beginning Class with a Laugh — 55
Offering–Encouraging Children to Give — 58

Worship–Entering into God's Presence	61
Object Lessons–Sermons that Connect with Kids	64
Puppets–A Fun Way to Minister	67
Powerful Sermons and Anointed Altar Calls	71
Storytelling–Ministry that Entertains	75
Crafts–Hands on Projects to Teach the Word	79
Drama–Captivating the Audience	82
Memory Verses–Creative Ways to Teach	84

Part III: Specialty Class Divisions

Nursery	93
Toddlers	97
Tips for Nursery and Toddler Teachers	102
Diaper Changing Procedures	104
Preschoolers	105
Children and Preteens	110
Demonstration of a Children and Preteen Class	112
Sample Schedules	116

Part IV: Preparing Children for Ministry

Encouraging Children to Minister	119
Training Children to Use Puppets in the Ministry	121
Developing a Drama Team	127
Dancing with a Purpose	132
Singing for the Lord	136
About the Authors	139

Acknowledgements

We are so blessed to have crossed paths many years ago. God ordered our footsteps, and we have traveled similar roads together. First, we give God all the glory for ordaining us to be children's ministers. There is no greater calling than to lead a child to Christ.

Second, we acknowledge our husbands, Rod and Mark. Thanks for the encouragement and support you gave us as we completed this work for God. We also thank our parents and children. You all have been right there, ministering with us.

Finally, thanks to all the children's ministers, pastors, teachers, and helpers who worked with us in the past and who work with us now. We could not have written this handbook without you. Ministry is about teamwork, and throughout the years, God has blessed us with so many wonderful people who share a similar vision.

God bless you!

Imparting a Vision for Children's Ministry

Train up a child in the way he should go and when he is old he will not depart from it. (Prov. 22:6) Children who are trained, at home and church, in the Word of God will not depart from it. That is a promise of God!

The purpose of children's ministry is to train children in the way they should go.

Jesus is the way, the truth, and the life. (John 14:6) Children should be trained in the Word of God, in the Spirit of God, and in the Power of God. Also, they should learn to pray, attend church faithfully, and live victorious lives.

The vision for each child should be that he/she is saved, guided by the Holy Spirit, listening to the voice of God, and having a strong personal relationship with God. Each child should know who he/she is in Christ Jesus, living a dedicated, committed, and victorious life in Him. Each child should be taught to be a mighty warrior in the kingdom of God, receiving and taking all the promises of God. Each child should accept nothing less than God's perfect will in every area of his/her life, always being blessed and becoming the blessing God intended.

The vision for children's teachers should be that each teacher is saved, totally committed, guided by the Holy Spirit, and listening to the voice of God. They should know fully who they are in Christ, blessed in every way and being a blessing to others. (Gen. 12:2) Teachers should be examples in love, word, and deed and in all ways to their young followers. (1 Tim. 4:12) Teachers should meet the spiritual, mental, physical, and emotional needs of their pupils in class and to be faithful to pray, study, and prepare for those pupils. Every teacher should touch those around them with the love of God, the Word of God, and the power of the Holy Spirit in them.

The vision for children's ministry should be for growth. Areas of growth should include the Word of God, the Anointing, developing spiritual fruits and gifts, and in number (Acts 2:47), as God added to them daily! God is *El Shaddai*, the God of more than enough, in every area of the ministry: more than enough materials, anointing, joy, strength, time, peace, creativity, finances, help, etc.

There should be a vision for a children's outreach ministry, ministering outside the church and touching the lives of others with puppets, dramas, dances, and choir songs. This helps prepare children to minister as adults without fear and inhibitions.

May all teachers and their children receive the blessings promised to those who continually teach the Word of God to their children (Deut. 11:19–21), that the days of their lives and the lives of their children will be multiplied and their days as heaven on earth. Count yourselves and all who work in children's ministry as blessed! *For children are a blessing of the Lord.* (Ps. 127:3)

May this book not only impart a vision for children's ministry, but also offer the needed assistance in attaining this vision for the teaching staff and the children being ministered to. May God bless you!

Part I
Foundations of a Children's Ministry

. . . .

Is There not a Cause for a Biblically Sound Children's Ministry?

I. We are commanded to teach and train children about God.

    A. God made his covenant with Abraham because God knew Abraham would command his children and his household to keep the way of the Lord. (Gen. 18:19)

    B. The people of Israel are commanded to train their children and teach them God's Word.

        1. Teach the children God's Word. (Deut. 4:10)

        2. Teaching children God's Word brings blessings and long life. (Deut. 6:1-3)

        3. Teach God's Word continually, and you'll receive these promises. (Deut. 6:5-7; 11:18-21)

            a. Your days will be multiplied.

            b. Your children's days will be multiplied.

       c. You and your children's days will be as heaven upon the earth.

   C. Joshua reminds the nation of Israel to train children. (Josh. 24:15)

   D. *All thy children shall be taught of the Lord, and great shall be thy peace.* (Isa. 54:13)

   E. *Train up a child in the way he should go, and when he is old, he will not depart from it.* (Prov. 22:6)

   F. Peter is commanded to "Feed my lambs." (John 21:15)

II. There is a cause. Children are valuable! *Children are a heritage of the Lord.* (Ps. 127:3)

   A. Jesus realized their value and ministered to them.

      1. He taught that kindness to children is rewarded by God. (Matt. 10:42)

      2. He taught his disciples to respect children and to not offend them. *Suffer little children and forbid them not to come unto me.* (Mark 10:13-16)

      3. Jesus took children in his arms and blessed them. (Mark 10:16)

      4. Jesus raised Jairus' daughter from the dead. (Luke 8:41-42; 8:49-56)

      5. Jesus cast the Devil out of the Canaanite woman's child. (Matt. 15:21-28)

      6. Jesus cast the Devil from a boy. (Matt. 17:14-18)

B. God realized the value of children and used them to accomplish His will.

1. David is a warrior in 1 Sam. 17:1-5 and a worship leader in 1 Sam. 16:19-23.

2. In 2 Kings 22:1 and 23:28, Josiah is a child king that turned Israel back to God.

3. Samuel hears the voice of the Lord in 1 Sam. 3:1,2.

4. In Isaiah 60:4, Isaiah prophecies that sons and daughters will come to the Lord.

5. In 2 Kings 5:1-4, Naaman hears the testimony of a child and is healed.

6. In Jer. 1:4-10, Jeremiah is called to prophesy as a child.

7. *Sons and daughters shall prophesy.* (Joel 2:28)

8. In Luke 2:41-52, Jesus began preparation for his ministry as a child.

9. Timothy is a young evangelist in 2 Tim. 1:6 and a pastor in 1 Tim. 4:12.

C. Satan realizes the value of children and attempts to destroy them.

1. *The thief cometh not but for to kill, steal, and to destroy.* (John 10:10)

2. Currently an estimated 4,000 abortions are performed daily.

D. Blessings and curses are based on the teaching of children.

1. Blessings came to those who trained their children, including Abraham, Isaac, the nation of Israel, King Josiah, Jehosophat, Moses, Samuel, and Timothy.

2. Curses or punishment came to parents and children when the children were not trained.

    a. Eli and his sons lost their lives and the right to be High Priests, and the presence of God was removed from the nation of Israel because Eli did not train his sons. (1 Sam. 2-4)

    b. Samuel's sons lost the right to become High Priests when Samuel did not train his sons in the ways of God. (1 Sam. 8:1-3)

    c. The nation of Israel always lost the blessings promised to them when the children were not trained in the ways of the Lord and thus began to follow false gods. (Isa. 1:4)

    d. Kings such as Ahab rose to power and curses came to the nation when the children were not trained in the ways of the Lord. (1 Kings 16:29-32)

    e. A heart of compassion and love for children are reasons for an emphasis on children's ministry.

III. All ministry is based on love.

    A. Jesus' ministry is based on love.

        1. *For God so loved that he gave...* (John 3:16)

        2. Jesus ministered out of compassion and love. (Matt. 9:36)

        3. Jesus loved and so he gave his life.

    B. We must love the children enough to

        1. Give selflessly.

        2. Desire to see them saved, sanctified, and led by God's Holy Spirit, boldly sharing the Gospel with others, and leading a victorious life.

        3. Minister out of compassion.

        4. Show that God's agape love is unconditional, unfailing, and never-ending.

IV. We are commissioned by Christ to take the Gospel of Jesus throughout the world to all ages. We are commissioned to teach the lost, heal the sick, and cast out devils.

    A. Jesus was first commissioned. (Luke 4:18)

    B. He then sent others with the "Great Commission," which basically says to preach the Gospel, heal the sick, and cast out devils.

        1. Jesus sent the twelve disciples. (Matt. 10:7, 8 and Mark 6:7–12)

        2. He sent the seventy men. (Luke 10:1–20)

3. He sent all believers. (Mark 16:15–18)

C. In John 21:15, Jesus told Peter first to "feed my lambs."

1. According to the Barna Group, fifty percent of all who are saved were saved before the age of thirteen and sixty-six percent were saved before age eighteen.

2. The Great Commission is to share the Gospel with all ages, but the under-eighteen group is a field particularly ripe for harvest.

D. *Now is the day of salvation.* (2 Cor. 6:2)

1. *God is...not willing that any should perish, but that all should come to repentance.* (2 Peter 3:9)

2. The Lord's return is soon!

3. Are you running to save the spiritually dead?

V. We are compelled by the need to minister to children.

A. Ministry brings rewards.

1. *Whosoever shall give to drink unto one of these little ones a cup of cold water only in the name of a disciple, verily I say unto you, he shall in no wise lose his reward.* (Matt. 10:42)

B. Applying the Scriptures in Matt. 25:34–40 to physical needs compels Christians to minister to not only the physical needs but also the spiritual needs of children of all ages.

1. The hungry are fed the Word of God.

      2. The thirsty are given a drink of the Spirit.

      3. Strangers are made part of the family of God.

      4. The naked are clothed in robes of righteousness.

      5. The sick (physically, emotionally, or spiritually) are visited and healed.

      6. Prisoners to sin are visited and set free.

  C. The world has made all kinds of attacks on children through abortion, child abuse, pornography, drugs, molestation, etc. These attacks have been designed to steal our youth's lives and their relationships with God. The church needs to feel this sense of urgency and be compelled to minister to these children.

VI. In 1 Sam. 17:29, when David's brothers taunted him for killing the giant, David replied "Is there not a cause?"

  A. We have been commanded, commissioned, and compelled to teach the children. We have been given compassion for them.

  B. Is there not a cause to teach and train children in God's Word?

Why Teach Children?

I. Why teach?

　A. Children are gifts from God and are valuable!

　B. *Lo, children are a heritage of the Lord; and the fruit of the womb is his reward.* (Ps. 127:3)

II. Whom to teach?

　A. The children. We should begin teaching them as babies and continue throughout their whole life.

　B. *Whom shall he teach knowledge? And whom shall he make to understand doctrine? Them that are weaned from the milk, and drawn from the breasts.* (Is. 28:9)

III. When to teach?

　A. Children should be taught the Word of God continually.

　B. *And thou shalt teach them diligently unto thy children, and shalt talk of them when thou sittest in thine house, and when thou walkest by the way, and when thou liest down, and when thou risest up.* (Deut. 6:7)

IV. How to teach?

　A. The Word of God must be planted in children's hearts by teaching God's Word. The Word should be nurtured to grow there to produce great blessings.

B. *The sower sowest the Word.* (Mark 4:14)

C. *Now the parable is this: the seed is the Word of God.* (Luke 8:11)

D. *Be not deceived; God is not mocked: for whatsoever a man soweth, that shall he also reap.* (Gal. 6:7)

E. *In the beginning was the Word, and the Word was with God, and the Word was God.* (John 1:1)

V. What to teach?

A. Children should be taught Christian foundations. They need to understand how to be saved and how to have a relationship with Him.

B. Children should know God as Creator and as a God of love. (Gen. 1 and 2, I John 4:7, 8)

C. Children should know God's salvation plan through Jesus. (John 3:16)

D. Children to know God in His fullness and have a personal relationship with Him. (I John 1:3, 4)

E. Children should know how to hear His voice and direction. (John 10:2, 5; 1 Kings 19:12, and Prov. 3:5, 6)

F. Children should know how to be a witness and the reason for witnessing. (Matt 5:15, 16 and Mark 15:15)

G. Children should know how to be heavenly or spiritually minded. (Matt. 16:27, 1 Cor. 3:8, Luke 23:41, and Rom. 8:6)

H. Children should know how to walk in the victory we've been given through Jesus Christ. (2 Cor. 2:14; 1 Cor. 15:57; John 10:10; and Gal. 3:13, 14)

How to Begin a Children's Ministry

I. Prayer.

    A. *The effectual fervent prayer of a righteous man availeth much.* (James 5:16)

    B. *Be careful for nothing; but in everything by prayer and supplication with thanksgiving let your requests be made known unto God.* (Phil. 4:6)

    C. *And this is the confidence that we have in him, that, if we ask any thing according to his will, he heareth us: And if we know that he hear us, whatsoever we ask, we know that we have the petitions that we desired of him.* (1 John 5:14, 15)

    D. *And all things, whatsoever ye shall ask in prayer, believing, ye shall receive.* (Matt. 21:22)

    E. Every children's ministry should be birthed in prayer.

II. The next step must always be good communication with the pastor.

    A. Allow the pastor to share his vision for children, and then you share yours.

    B. You will find that most pastors are supportive of children's ministry.

    C. Often pastors see the importance of this ministry but

simply do not have the time, knowledge, or help to begin such an enormous task.

D. Pastors are generally appreciative of anyone who is willing to accept the responsibility of this great calling.

E. If the pastor is not supportive, pray for him to have a heart for children and a vision for children's ministry.

F. Remember to catch the pastor's vision so to continue the same vision within the children's ministry.

G. Determine the rules and regulations that must be implemented. Like all ministries in the church, the children's ministry must submit to the pastor's leadership and to the church's vision.

III. Basic foundations for getting started:

A. Begin with prayer.

1. With the pastor and with others interested in beginning this ministry, pray for a clear vision and direction.

2. Pray for specific vision and direction.

3. *Write the vision, make it plain upon the tables that he may run that readeth it.* (Hab. 2:2)

4. Pray for materials, finances, etc. necessary to do the Lord's work with the children.

B. Survey the number and ages of the children in the church to determine the classes needed most.

C. Survey the number of people interested in helping as teachers, classroom helpers, members of an outside support group, and those who will help only on special events and programs.

D. Survey the special talents and anointings available. Much of this can be revealed only through prayer.

E. Determine the number of rooms available and the size of these rooms.

F. Knowing whether there are several very small rooms, a few larger rooms, or a combination of large and small rooms will help determine class divisions.

G. Survey the materials available.

1. Are there materials, supplies, decorations, and most of all literature?

2. What age is this appropriate for?

3. Is there anything usable, or is it in bad shape, too outdated, etc?

4. You might also check with the church members to see if anyone is interested in donating items you may need.

   a. Items for nursery and toddler classes are often available and readily donated as children outgrow these items.

   b. Items to ask for include: playpen, crib bed, toddler toys, rocker, changing tables, small chairs, CD players, TVs, etc.

H. Determine class organization and divisions compiled by using the information that has been gathered.

1. Determine the number of classes you can have based on the number of children, number of teachers available, and the number and size of the rooms available.

2. It is usually best to have at least two teachers in each class.

3. A teacher and an assistant can divide the workload, double the prayer and preparation time, and assist one another in problems. Having two teachers also will keep the class moving at a faster pace with less dead time between activities, thereby eliminating many behavior problems, etc.

4. Begin with the number of classes that best fits your situation. Add classes as the number of teachers and pupils grow.

5. The more children the greater the number of classes and the smaller the division of ages. The following are examples of division for classes:

    a. One class only—Children ages 4-12 years

    b. Two classes—Children ages 2-5 and 6-10 years

    c. Three classes—Children 2-4, 5-8, and 9-12 years

    d. Four classes—Children 0-1, 2-4, 5-8, and 9-12 years

    e. Six Classes—Children 0-1, 2-3, 4-5, 6-7, 8-10, and 11-12 years

    f. Remember: These are only sample divisions and must be adapted to fit your church and children's needs.

I. Choose literature that is appropriate for each class.

1. Once the decisions are made regarding the number of classes, the age divisions, and the teachers, begin to choose literature that is age-appropriate, easy to use, and based on the biblical word.

2. The literature should be doctrinally sound.

3. It needs to be age-appropriate.

4. It should teach a central thought and theme from the Word.

5. It should include a Bible story and should contain supplemental lessons, such as stories, objects lessons, dramas, puppet skits, coloring sheets, etc. that reinforce the same central theme.

6. Changing themes often in one class can be confusing to children; therefore, literature that does this should not be used.

J. Next, the director needs to meet with teachers and aides to train all the workers.

1. This manual can be helpful in training workers.

2. Encourage teachers and aides to attend any local teacher-training workshops or seminars.

3. If there are no workshops available, train by using this handbook.

4. Teachers who have been trained have a greater success, enjoy teaching more, and will stay committed longer.

5. One large workshop followed by monthly 'in-touch' and training meetings will be helpful to keep teachers informed and refreshed.

K. Once everything else is organized, decorate the classroom based on the age of the pupils, the literature being used, or perhaps the season.

1. Classrooms should be bright, colorful, and inviting.

2. Classrooms should be clean, neat, and organized.

L. Gather the material needed in each classroom, such as furniture, equipment, and music, to supply each teacher's class.

1. This will enable the teacher to do an effective job ministering to the children in their classroom.

2. Encourage input from the teachers as to the needs in the class.

3. Arrange a 'wish list' with the most necessary items first.

4. Then begin acquiring the items needed. Begin with the most needed items first and add to the class as availability allows.

IV. You are now ready to begin.

A. Do not despise small beginnings.

B. Trust God, and watch the growth in every area.

C. Make adjustments as necessary.

D. Growth and time always bring change, requiring continual self-evaluation and adjustments to continue meeting the needs of the children.

Planning for Success

I. *We may make our plans, but God has the last word.* (Prov. 16:1, Good News Bible)

    A. When we know what God wants us to do, then we can have total confidence that what we are attempting to do is right and that God is on our side.

II. The old saying "Failing to plan is planning to fail" is very true, especially with children's ministry.

    A. Ideas go away, but direction stays.

    B. Successful children's ministry must have someone who is willing to plan and to direct the staff and the children's ministry as a whole.

    C. Sometimes tasks seem impossible, but with God, all things are possible. (Luke 1:37)

    D. Even Jesus planned. He had he disciples seat the crowd in groups of fifty and hundreds. (Mark 6:32-44)

III. Planning for success is inevitable when you remember: *If God be for us, who can be against us?"* (Rom. 8:31)

    A. Knowing your position in Christ will always bring success. (2 Cor. 2:14)

    B. *Any enterprise is built by wise planning and becomes strong common sense and profits wonderfully by keeping abreast of the facts.* (Prov. 24:3-5, Living Bible)

IV. Trust in God and in your covenant with Him.

   A. Just as did David, who saw Goliath as a loser even though the whole army (Israel) was shaking in their boots (sandals). David knew his covenant with God would make him a winner, even in an apparent 'no-win' situation.

   B. Possible 'no-win' situations you may face are:

   1. Lack of workers

   2. Lack of support from the senior pastor

   3. Classroom condition

   4. The size of classrooms

   5. Behavior problems.

   C. Any of these situations could become your Goliath or giant, defying your hope (confident expectation) in your children's ministry. Instead, just do what David did.

   1. Goliath laughed and scorned, but David replied:
   I come to you in the name of the Lord of hosts, the God of the armies of Israel, whom you have defied. This day will the Lord deliver you into my hands! (1 Sam. 17:45)

   2. David had a king's heart before he became the king.

   3. He made this decree with confidence: *The Lord*

  doesn't save you with a spear and a sword, for the battle is the Lord's, and he will give you into our hands. (1 Sam. 17:47)

V. Whatever you are called to do, God will equip you to do it.

 A. When God called Moses, he anointed him and equipped him.

  1. For every excuse Moses had, God had an answer. When Moses complained, "I can't speak plain," God sent Aaron.

  2. God empowered Moses to send and remove the plagues and part the Red Sea.

  3. God anointed Moses to hear God's voice.

  4. God sent what Moses needed to accomplish the job he was called to do, such as the staff and people with hearts like Aaron to help.

 B. When God gives you an assignment, he gives you the anointing to carry it out and grace to help in time of need.

 C. Trust in the Lord, always expecting him to direct you and give you wisdom. (Prov. 3:5, 6)

Recruiting Staff

I. How do I get workers?

    A. Pray. Prayer is the number-one recruiting tool!

    B. The Lord will give you the desires of your heart. *Delight thyself also in the Lord: and he shall give thee the desires of thine heart.* (Ps. 37:4)

    C. Believe that you have received your answer and thank God for it daily. (Mark 11:24)

    D. Actions speak louder than words. Therefore, your attitude will speak either blessings or curses about your children's ministry.

    E. Negative example: If you say, "We never have enough help," you are planting a negative confession over your ministry.

    F. Positive example: You need to say, "I believe we have more than enough help." You are blessing your ministry with such confessions.

    G. When you talk to people, be careful what you say about your ministry. You may have had a hard night with thirty children, but you still need to make a positive confession.

    H. You are the best recruiter for your ministry. Share

with others the exciting things going on in children's ministry and the joy in fulfilling your call in this ministry.

II. How do I keep teachers?

A. Train them.

B. If you want teachers to stay with your department, you need to mentor them.

C. If you just throw a new teacher into class and say, "Here is our lesson, go to it," then most likely that teacher will last one night!

D. Jesus trained his disciples.

E. We need to train our teachers. This develops confidence and ability.

F. If the secular world trains its employees, then how much more should teachers with children be trained?

III. Training

A. Allow the person to observe class.

1. Afterward, allow him/her to talk to you, and listen to the person's thoughts.

2. Find out what peaked his/her interest.

B. Allow the new teacher to do one part of class.

1. Always be an example by demonstration, not only to the class, but to your new teacher as well.

C. Show your new teacher where to find all the materials.

1. The goal of training your teachers is to have them become just like you!

IV. What should I do about high absenteeism?

   A. With a training program, you will always be working with new teachers.

   B. When you get your core teachers trained, they immediately begin to train and recruit. Every trained teacher should always be training.

   C. We have teachers and teacher's assistants.

   D. God gives every one of us gifts and talents, and each teacher can contribute an important part to the class.

   E. When a teacher is absent, the other teachers in the class should be trained enough to carry on with class.

   F. Every teacher and teacher's assistant should have a copy of the curriculum and a monthly schedule.

V. Teamwork

   A. Children's ministry is not a one-man show. It is a team effort!

   B. It doesn't matter if your church is large or small, you need someone to assist you and work with you. Then you both can begin to train others.

   C. Keep a positive attitude! If you feel frustrated, go pray.

      1. If you can't get past it, get someone to pray with you.

      2. Don't quit!

      3. God places children's ministry on the hearts of only a few special people. The Devil would love to discourage you, but be encouraged.

      4. The call to teach is without repentance! (Rom. 11:29)

Organizing for Growth

I. Organization is necessary to prepare for growth in children's ministry.

    A. You cannot grow past the number of children you can handle.

    B. The better organized you are, the more effectively you can minister to large numbers.

    C. The larger a ministry grows, the more organized it must become to meet the spiritual needs of each child.

II. Organize each departmental class:

    A. By age and common characteristics

    B. According to space available

    C. According to the number of workers available

III. Record-keeping report systems are necessary to prepare for ministry to larger numbers of children.

    A. The following reports should be compiled and turned into the children's pastor monthly:

        1. Attendance reports

        2. Offering reports

3. Expenditure reports

B. A child information sheet should be filed in each class.

C. Teachers should answer questionnaires and fill out commitment sheets stating the expectations required. *Know those who labor among you.* (1 Thes. 5:12)

D. Each department should have a three-ring binder containing:

1. Teachers' names, addresses, and phone numbers
2. Children's information sheets with names, parents names, address, phone number, birth date, grade, and other types of information, such as allergies
3. Schedules
4. Teachers' commitment sheets
5. Copies of all records
6. Any training materials used
7. Any special information particular to that department or class

E. Each department should have record-keeping sheets particular to the age being ministered to.

1. For example, the nursery needs a record of information such as when the baby was last fed, what feeding schedule the child is on, what method of feeding the baby is receiving, etc.
2. There also needs to be a chart to register when

the baby was last fed and changed, so the parents can be informed when they return to pick up the child. This information is particular to the nursery class, but there are different facts particular to other age groups.

F. A weekly attendance chart with each child's name on it should be kept. If a child misses two or three services, contact can be made by phone or postcard or in person.

G. Monthly schedules should be turned in to the children's pastor.

1. This will help ensure a balance between adult services and children's ministry for all teachers and will help to locate a substitute worker who might trade on the schedule to cover for another teacher's absence.

IV. Literature pacing guides

A. Have an annual schedule for the literature being used in every department.

B. This schedule will be used to look at the curriculum so that the children's pastor will know what each department is teaching.

C. This also helps prevent departments from teaching the same curriculum simultaneously.

The Teacher Image

General or public perception, likeness, or representation

I. Be a Godly image.

    A. Men and women are created in God's image.

        1. *Let us make man in our image after our likeness. So God created he him, male and female created he them.* (Gen. 1:26, 27)

        2. We are restored after sin by the blood of Christ.

    B. Jesus was the image of God. In John 5:19, 20 and Col. 1:15, Jesus is the image of the invisible God.

    C. *Lest the light of the glorious Gospel of Christ, who is the image of God, should shine unto them.* (2 Cor. 4:4)

    D. Jesus told his disciples (we are disciples also) to follow (imitate) him.

    E. *If any man serve me, let him follow me.* (John 12:26 and Matt. 4:19)

    F. *As we have borne the image of the earthy, we shall also bear the image of the heavenly.* (1 Cor. 15:49)

II. Be an example.

    A. Christ was our example. *Forever here unto were ye called because Christ also suffered for us, leaving us an example, that ye should follow his steps.* (1 Pet. 2:21)

    B. Paul stated he was an example in 2 Tim 2:2 and 1 Tim 1:16. *Those things which ye have both learned and received and heard and seen in me do, and the God of peace shall be with you.* (Phil. 4:9)

    C. *In all things shewing thyself a pattern of good works; in doctrine shewing incorruptness, gravity, sincerity, sound speech, that cannot be condemned; that he that is of the contrary part may be ashamed, having no evil thing to say to you.* (Tit. 2:7-8)

    D. *Feed the flock of God which is among you, taking the oversight thereof, not of constraint, but willingly; not for filthy lucre, but of a ready mind; neither as being lords over God heritage, but being ensamples of the flock.* (1 Peter 5:2-3)

    E. *Let no man despise thy youth; but be thou an example of the believers.* (1 Tim. 4:12)

        1. In word (Col. 3:16, 2 Tim. 2:15, and Ps. 119:130)

        2. In conversation (2 Tim. 2:16; Matt. 12:36, 37; and Prov. 6:2, 10:19, 15:2, 6:24, and 25:11)

        3. In charity or love (Eph. 5:1, 1 Cor. 13:1, and 1 Tim. 2:15)

        4. In spirit (2 Cor. 12:18 and 2 Cor. 3:17, 18)

        5. In faith (Heb. 6:12 and Heb. 13:7)

        6. In purity (Deut. 16:20, 1 Tim. 6:11, and 2 Tim. 2:22)

III. Be the authority. Jesus taught as one having authority in Mark 1:27.

   A. Provide a teachable environment.

      1. State rules and be willing to enforce them, thereby providing security and peace for the children.

      2. Every student has the right to receive from God's Word and the Holy Spirit.

      3. Be humble, loving, and kind, yet firm.

   B. Set the mood for the class.

      1. Always be warm, friendly, and loving.

      2. Provide times to laugh and play.

      3. Always give love, hugs, and attention.

   C. Make the classroom colorful, clean, decorated, and welcoming. It represents God's house to the children.

   D. Teachers should wear a smile, be neat, clean, and dressed appropriately, for they are the image of God to their students.

IV. Be excellent!

   A. *The disciple is not above his master; but everyone that is perfect shall be as his master.* (Luke 6:40)

   B. Being excellent means you make the most of what you have and strive to become better every day.

Encouraging Students To Be Their Best

I. Implementing the following steps will help establish and maintain class control.

    A. Implementing the 'Three Ps' (prayer, plans, and preparation) will prevent behavior problems.

    B. Pray for love, forgiveness, wisdom, peace, joy, obedience, the anointing of the Holy Ghost, etc. to be a part of each class of students. Pray for each segment of the class to be effective.

    C. Plan for a successful class.

    D. Prepare for each segment of the class by studying faithfully the lesson and having all the materials ready for use.

II. Teachers should:

    A. Establish a relationship based on love. Keep a loving atmosphere within the classroom.

    B. Make learning a fun experience to prevent problems from arising.

    C. Make class fun, exciting, interesting, and fast-paced.

    D. Be aware of the attention span of the age group to

which you are ministering.

E. Do not violate the children's attention because this can lead to problems. A child's attention span is approximately one minute per year of age; therefore, each segment of the lesson should not be longer than one minute per year of age, of the average age of the students in the class.

F. Teach on the children's level.

G. Teach lessons and materials that are age-appropriate.

H. Have reasonable expectations of acceptable behavior for the age you teach. *When I was a child, I spake as a child, I understood as a child, [and] I thought as a child.* (1 Cor. 13:11)

I. Have rules and regulations that are:

1. Stated simply.

2. Stated positively.

3. Applied consistently.

J. Be the authority, being firm when necessary. Make sure your body language agrees with your words. Remember—being firm is not being hateful, but is being sincere.

K. Give incentives to encourage appropriate behavior.

L. Reward good behavior.

M. Encourage children to be their best.

1. *But whoso shall offend one of these little ones which*

believe in me, it were better for him that a millstone were hanged about his neck, and that he were drowned in the depth of the sea. (Matt. 18:6)

2. *And, ye fathers, provoke not your children to wrath: but bring them up in the nurture and admonition of the Lord.* (Eph. 6:4)

3. Speak positively.

4. Expect the best from every child.

5. Smile often.

6. Maintain eye contact.

7. Give the children responsibilities.

8. Stay alert to potential behavior problems, and plan ahead to prevent these from occurring.

III. Techniques for handling misbehavior

A. Remain calm—*don't* overreact. When you lose self-control, you've already lost control of your class.

B. If the behavior is not disruptive, ignore it.

C. Refocus attention from bad behavior to good behavior by:
1. A look
2. A nod of the head
3. A touch
4. Speaking the child's name. If you are teaching, this

can be done by saying several children's names in the story, including the child who is unfocused.

D. Disruptive behavior that persists needs to be addressed in a more direct manner, with as little attention as possible drawn to it and without embarrassing anyone.

E. Be firm. Use an authoritative voice, and be sure your body language agrees with your words.

F. Avoid sarcasm and idle threats.

G. Administer correction in love. Know the pupil well enough to know what is effective with that child.

H. Correct immediately, when possible. Have the teacher who is not teaching at the time handle any situation or disruption immediately and quietly.

IV. Discipline

A. When possible, let the punishment fit the crime. An example is when a child intentionally makes a mess—he/she can spend free time cleaning up the mess.

B. Below are six progressive steps to take when handling a situation or bad behavior. Only progress to the next step when the preceding one fails.

1. Correct by words.

2. Correct by relocation in the class.

3. Correct by isolation from the group.

4. Correct by removal from the class. Contact the coordinator.

5. Contact the children's pastor.

6. The children's pastor may contact the church pastor, and parents of the child may be contacted for a conference in order to enlist the parents' aid and to assist them in any areas in which they may need help. Parents and teachers working together with the support of the Lord can turn everything around.

C. Practice and develop your sense of humor. It will make teaching and class more fun.

D. Always keep your students' actions in perspective. Do not overreact to situations.

E. Degrading remarks are inappropriate and will do more damage than good.

F. Correct—then forgive.

G. If the problem persists, begin to search for underlying causes.

H. Remember that love never fails. Loving discipline rather than harsh punishment is basic for good behavior.

Planning and Organizing Big Events

I. Planning—*For I know the plans I have or you, says the Lord. They are plans for good and not for evil, to give you a future and hope.* (Jer. 29:11)

   A. Vision

   1. Begin with a vision for the project, establishment, ministry, or activity.

   2. *Where there is no vision, the people perish.* (Prov. 29:18)

   3. If you do not impart the vision for an undertaking, no one can follow or assist you.

   4. Without a vision, the ministry will die.

   5. The Dead Sea is dead because nothing flows in or out of it. A ministry must have a vision and direction imparted into it in order for ministry and accomplishments to come from it. A ministry without a vision becomes stifled and dies.

   6. *Write the vision and make it plain upon tables, that he may run that readeth it.* (Hab 2:2)

   7. Make the vision plain to all who are a part of it. Share the vision and the information available.

8. Point directions for each one to run toward. Give any available facts to support the vision and help give direction to those who are willing to become a part of it.

B. Plans—*Any enterprise is built by wise planning, becomes strong through common sense, and profits wonderfully by keeping abreast of the facts.* (Prov. 24:3, 4 *Living Bible*)

1. Prayer is always the basis for all plans. You must hear from God! John 10:4 says, *And when he putteth forth his own sheep, he goeth before them, and the sheep follow him: for they know his voice.*

2. Gather all the facts and information obtainable from previous experiences or events and from others.

3. Use common sense. We have the mind of Christ so we have good sense and the ability to make practical and logical decisions.

C. Planning is always a step of faith. Be willing to try new ideas if you have peace when you pray. Always pray and follow the peace of God.

D. Planning is worth the time it takes.

E. Planning is essential to organizing any area of ministry.

F. If you fail to plan, you are planning to fail.

II. Organizing—Putting the right people, in the right place, at the right time doing the right things, in the right way, with the right equipment to achieve the right results.

A. The right people—Choose people based on anointing, calling, willingness, dependability, faithfulness and abilities. Abilities and anointing without willingness, faithfulness, and dependability are wasted. (Prov. 25:19)

B. The right place—Example: Put someone who loves art and is talented in charge of doing the artistic work and someone who is a great cook in charge of the kitchen and food services.

C. The right time—There is a perfect timing with God.

1. Pray first and then schedule the event or activity on the best date and time.

2. Always gather the facts first, such as other scheduled events in the church, communities, and schools and of those who are working with you.

3. Also pray and plan a schedule of events, allowing the projects to flow smoothly from one activity to another.

D. The right thing—Just because that is the way it has been done before doesn't mean it has to be repeated. If something works, don't fix it, but if areas didn't work before, change them! Always add new ideas. Even things that work can grow old.

E. The right way—Each person working corporately as a team, giving and receiving help without offense.

1. Choose department heads for each major area of work to be accomplished.

2. Each department head is responsible for his/her area, working with the team to achieve the

desired results.

3. Each department head reports to the director, keeping the director completely informed regarding all major decisions and actions. The only way any endeavor can have success and unity is if the director is kept abreast of the facts, to bring continuity, flow, and organization between the departments.

4. Having regular meetings among all department heads and the director to report progress and to continue to promote unity.

F. The right equipment

1. Have the department heads make a list of any material and equipment they need to succeed in their assigned area.

2. Make a list of any general items needed to accomplish the project or event.

3. Designate someone to purchase or order the needed materials.

G. The right results—A successful event or project is well planned and organized, running smoothly from one activity to another (without chaos or confusion), with all the people working as a team to achieve a common goal with the right material and decorations to enhance and meet the needs of all involved.

Promotion of Big Events

I. The promotion of big events can really make a difference in the attendance at them.

    A. Take something simple and make it look really big to children.

    B. Some examples are:

        1. The World's Largest Popsicle—Purchase a 32-gallon trash can, sterilize it, and then fill it with Kool-Aid. Place a 2x4 through the lid for the stick. Cut a hole in the lid to stabilize the stick. Place the can in a stand-up freezer. Allow it to freeze for several days.

        2. The World's Largest Banana Split—Take a new child-size swimming pool and create a banana split by using three large containers of ice cream. Have nuts, bananas, and various toppings surrounding the ice cream. Be sure to separate the toppings so children can choose their preference. Each child gets a separate bowl of the banana split. This is very appealing to children.

II. Great promotions attract a crowd.

    A. Tantalizing prizes are always great incentives.

    B. Example prizes that have worked well are:

       1. Bicycles

       2. Cash

       3. Games systems

       4. Flat-screen TVs

       5. iPods

III. Promotion of any event is a necessity.

    A. Play it up big in every class.

    B. Have the pastor mention it in regular church services prior to the event.

    C. Show off the prizes. Example: ride the bicycle through the church during the announcement of the event.

    D. Interview the children, asking them what they would do with the prize.

    E. Have a competition between boys and girls.

IV. Advertising

    A. Contact local newspapers, radio stations, social media, and TV stations.

    B. Colorful flyers placed in prime locations will help inform the community of the upcoming event.

       1. Place flyers at eye level.

       2. Make the flyer eye-catching.

       3. Use large icons.

V. Planning the big event is essential to success.

    A. Begin with a central theme.

    B. Have an initial meeting.

    C. Use an organizing outline.

    D. Appoint someone to be in charge of the big event.

Sample Itemized Director's List for Large Events
Kids' Crusade, Hallelujah Night, Etc.

Directors: _____

1. Title and Theme: _____
2. Date and Time: _____
3. Advertisements: _____
    - o   Brochures
    - o   Posters
    - o   Flyers
    - o   Post Cards
    - o   Newspaper
    - o   Radio
    - o   TV
4. Literature: _____
    - o   Write or Purchase
    - o   Who will teach, what they will teach, when they will teach etc.
    - o   Lesson schedules, etc.
    - o   Teacher schedules
5. Music: _____
    - o   Children
    - o   Adults
    - o   Choir
    - o   Dance
6. Extra Ministry: _____
    - o   Puppet
    - o   Drama
    - o   Dance

7. Food: _____
   o   Preparation
   o   People to serve
   o   Food items
8. Van Ministry: _____
   o   Drivers
   o   Routes
9. Registration Tables: _____

10. Decorations: _____

11. Purchasing Needed Material and Prizes: _____

12. Clean Up: _____

13. Make Schedule of the Activities for the Event: _____

14. Generate and Distribute Copies of Schedule (one for each worker):
_____

Class Promotion

I. Promotion to the next class division

    A. Every year, children look forward to the excitement of moving ahead to the next level. In school, they move to the next grade.

    B. Church should be no different. Your class departments and age divisions should depend on the size of your church and the number of children.

    C. As you begin the division of groups, you need to realize that this is a big step. Some parents want siblings to remain together. Over the years, we have seen many opposing factors in class division.

    D. The apostle Paul established positions within a governing body in the church. We have to have guidelines and rules, and as your church grows, the necessity for class divisions becomes greater.

II. When we began our ministry, we had two divisions: Children (3-10 years) and Teens (11 years and older). This was because these were the only Sunday School rooms we had available. As we grew in the numbers of children and rooms, we added more classes. We divided as follows:

    A. Newborn to age 1 year—Nursery

    B. Ages 1 year (or walking) to 3 years (potty-trained)—Toddler

    C. Age 3 years until completion of pre-kindergarten—Preschool

    D. Kindergarten through first grade—Beginners

    E. Second through fourth grades—Children's Church

    F. Fifth through seventh grades—Preteens

    G. Eighth grade through college—Teens

III. Class promotion allows teachers and parents to know exactly when their child moves to the next class. Usually, one service per year is devoted to the ceremony of class promotion.

IV. Ceremony for class promotion

    A. The children's director usually opens the service and introduces the nursery coordinator.

    B. The nursery coordinator welcomes all the babies born during the year and presents each with a certificate.

    C. The nursery coordinator introduces the toddler coordinator, and he/she stands on the opposite side of the platform.

    D. As the children's director calls each child's name, the nursery coordinator presents each child that is one year old and walking with a certificate of completion. We usually make these on the computer.

- E. The toddler coordinator receives the child either with a hug or by handing the child to the new teacher.
- F. As each coordinator finishes, he/she introduces the next department coordinator.
- G. Finally, after all coordinators have been introduced and all children have crossed the platform to their new teachers, the children's director or pastor closes the ceremony.
- H. We allow the children, Preschool through Preteen, to be promoted on a designated Sunday in June.
- I. Nursery children officially go to the toddler class when they are one year old and can walk confidently. Toddlers are promoted when they are three years old and are potty-trained.
- J. Toddlers visit their new class for about twenty minutes the week or two before their promotion. This helps the children adjust through the transition a little more easily.

V. Notes regarding the ceremony itself

- A. This can be a simple ceremony or very elaborate.
- B. The stage is the main setting for the ceremony, so you may want to decorate with graduation décor. Since it is a children's event, we usually use lots of balloons and streamers.
- C. The ceremony can also include special songs, poems, or musical solos.

D. You want all your children to attend, so you may want to send special invitations to your parents and grandparents.

E. Videos are always a special memento.

F. A typed program with a list of the children being promoted is a nice touch.

G. A baptismal service can be planned for after the ceremony for those children who want to be baptized.

H. Refreshments can be served afterwards, as a fun time of fellowship.

The Responsibilities of a Children's Pastor

I.. A children's pastor is a person who is called into the ministry of pastoring, but who is sent to the children.

   A. Jesus is the best example of a pastor.

   B. He discipled the twelve who worked with Him directly, while shepherding the flock. Yet, He continued in total submission to the Father God, working in congruence with the Spirit of God.

   C. Jesus was not able to minister personally to everyone himself while walking as a man on the earth, so he trained the twelve disciples and another seventy men.

   D. It is necessary for the children's pastor to impart the vision for the ministry to others who have a call and a desire to minister to children.

   E. In the beginning, when the ministry is small, a children's pastor may be able to minister to the children, train all the workers directly, organize and carry out all special events, etc.

   F. As the ministry increases in size, it will become essential to have anointed, trained, and dependable personnel to assist and coordinate in many areas.

This will allow for growth in the ministry.

G. For this reason, being a disciple to the children's workers is as important as is ministering to the children directly.

H. As a whole, the staff will have more frequent direct contact with each individual child in a particular age level than will the pastor, who will be ministering some at all age levels or departments.

I. Therefore, the children's pastor's duties include responsibility to God, the senior pastor, the children's ministry staff, the children, and even to the church and the parents.

II. The responsibilities of a children's pastor are:

A. To submit to God.

1. Spending time praying, studying the Word of God, listening to his voice, and submitting to his will is of the utmost importance! We can do nothing without him! (John 5:19)

B. To submit to and assist the senior pastor of the church.

1. To submit to the senior pastor's authority.

2. To know the senior pastor's vision for the church and to support and promote this vision.

3. To know the senior pastor's vision for the children's ministry and to implement this vision or press toward it.

4. To share his/her visions and plans for the

ministry for the senior pastor's approval before implementation.

5. To keep the senior pastor informed of all major activities, ministry changes, plans, etc.

6. To carry the responsibility of the children's ministry for the senior pastor, so he will never be encumbered by this area of the ministry.

7. To bring respect to God, to the senior pastor, and to the church by the way each matter is handled, each class is taught, the way the children's pastor conducts himself/herself in and out of church, etc.

8. To be faithful in attending all church services and functions.

9. To worship regularly. Children's pastors must have at least one service per week in the chapel to stay connected to God, to the pastor, and to the church.

C. To assist and disciple coordinators, assistant coordinators, teachers, and the entire children's ministry staff.

1. To plan, organize, and coordinate all major activities or to oversee the planning, etc. of these activities.

2. To organize for growth.

3. To promote teamwork among and within departments.

4. To keep each worker informed of scheduled church and children's ministry events.

5. To have regular in-touch meetings.

6. To be available to assist in any area needing help in resolving any problems.

7. To visit and participate in classes regularly.

8. To pray regularly for each class and each worker.

9. To visit each class before service for corporate prayer and to check for needs or assistance.

10. To oversee the implementation of the total program, from birth through grade seven.

D. To shepherd and minister to the children.

1. To teach and preach the Word of God and to oversee the teaching and preaching of the Word of God.

2. To be the keeper of their souls.

3. To evaluate the curriculum, making necessary purchases of curriculum and corresponding materials to meet the spiritual needs of the children.

4. To counsel and pray with children who have special needs.

5. To lead in children's revivals.

6. To pray for children and minister to them when led to by the Spirit.

7. To contact the children who have been absent for a designated period of time, after the coordinators and teachers have contacted the

child with no results.

8. To be responsible for home and hospital visitations.

9. To have good record-keeping charts in order to stay informed.

10. To personally minister to the children on a regular basis, in order to stay connected and shepherd the flock.

E. To oversee recruiting and training new workers.

1. Must meet all new recruits.

2. Must research and do a background check before allowing any new worker into the ministry to children.

3. Must have all new recruits approved by the senior pastor.

4. Must oversee the implementation of training new recruits. The assistant director implements the training of new recruits in conjunction with the coordinator of the department into which the new worker will enter.

5. Must schedule regular training sessions for new recruits and refresher courses for seasoned teachers.

F. To be the contact between the children's ministry and the parents and church.

1. To promote good relations between the children's ministry workers and the parents and church family.

2. To keep parents informed of upcoming events and of any special need of their child.

3. To meet with parents concerning any situation that involves their child.

4. To promote the vision for children's ministry in the church, from the pulpit, in the bulletins, with the parents, etc.

G. Children's pastors are part of the five-fold ministry.

1. *And he gave some, apostles; and some prophets; and some evangelists; and some pastors and teachers; for the perfecting of the saints, for the working of the ministry, for the edifying of the body of Christ.* (Eph. 4:11, 12)

2. Children's pastors should be mature Christians, strong in the Word and Spirit, experienced in working with children, people of integrity, respected in the church and community as people of good report, etc.

3. They are representatives of God, the pastor and the church in this office.

4. Children's pastors often operate as apostles, prophets, evangelists, and teachers when there is a need for these offices, but their primary function is as pastor to the children.

Coordinator Responsibilities

I. The responsibilities of the coordinator are:

   A. To minister to the children

   B. To oversee the department placed in his/her care

II. To support:

   A. The pastor

   B. The church's vision

   C. God's overall plan for the church

   D. The children's ministry director through prayer

   E. The children's ministry, by being willing to help with or plan any event

III. To report essential information to the children's director:

   A. All planned events, such as field trips

   B. Prospective new teachers and helpers

   C. Any situation that needs attention in his/her department

IV. To pray:

A. Shares corporate prayer with teachers and children before each class

B. Encourages teamwork for a ministry that is pleasing to God

V. To oversee:

A. Oversee the progress of his/her staff.

B. Assist in recruiting and training all new teachers.

C. Make certain each week that the teachers and helpers are prepared with curriculum, crafts, snacks and all teaching supplies.

D. Inform the director of any needs or desires that will enhance the training of the children.

E. Distribute copies of schedules to all teaches and helpers.

F. Delegate responsibilities for staff to call for replacement workers, when necessary.

VI. To attend meetings:

A. To stay informed

B. To relay information to everyone in his/her department

VII. To keep accurate records:

A. In class attendance

B. In offering

C. In expenditures

D. To give information to the children's ministry director

VIII. To be an example:

A. In lifestyle

B. In faith

C. In conduct of character

IX. To maintain classrooms by:

A. Keeping them colorfully decorated

B. Keeping them neat and clean

C. Keeping them well-organized

X. To constantly evaluate the effectiveness of the entire department by:

A. Praying for the department continually

B. Seeking God's will for the children and staff continually

C. Making changes when and where needed

Part II
Ministry in the Classroom

....

Ice Breakers—
Beginning Class with a Laugh

I. First impressions are very important. Not only should you and your class look neat in appearance, but how you begin says a lot about the class.

    A. Most ministers begin their sermon with a comment, or 'ice breaker,' that causes people to loosen up or just laugh.

    B. Children's ministry is no different. Some children:

        1. May be shy

        2. Feel uncomfortable leaving Mom and Dad

        3. May be visiting the church for the first time

        4. May be visiting from another church

II. Laughter brings unity.

    A. Humor allows children to relax.

    B. Laughter makes you feel comfortable.

III. Ideas for breaking the ice

A. Puppets are great.

   1. A puppet can enter telling a joke to the teacher.
   2. Two puppets can enter telling jokes, being mischievous, etc.
   3. The puppets can be dressed in weird costumes.
   4. The puppet can bring an odd object to show the teacher.
   5. The puppets can sing a crazy song.

B. Comical costume characters are great for ice breakers.

C. Plan to have the same character visit each week at the beginning of class.

   1. Examples are a clown, an old man, and a baby and store-bought characters, such as a gorilla, dog, etc.
   2. The characters may:

      a. Tell funny jokes to the teacher
      b. Tell funny jokes to the children
      c. Bring out strange objects to show the children
      d. Act silly
      e. Sing a funny tune

IV. Ice breakers have a purpose.

A. They bring the class into unity so the teacher can begin class.

        B. They can be used to introduce the rules in a funny way.

        C. They can be used to make announcements about upcoming events.

        D. They can encourage children to participate in contests.

V. Try using ice breakers.

        A. You may find children can't wait to get to class.

        B. You may have fun also!

Offerings—Encouraging Children to Give

I. Offerings can be a vital part of each service.

   A. It is essential that our children be taught the importance of tithing and giving while they are very young.

   B. *Train up a child in the way he should go and when he is old, he will not depart from it.* (Prov. 22:6)

II. Offerings show obedience to God.

   A. Children need to be taught that tithing and giving are in obedience to God's commandments.

   B. It is a form of worship to God.

   C. Giving opens the way for God to bless his people.

   D. Never ignore the importance of teaching God's Word about tithing and giving. *Will a man rob God? Yet ye have robbed me. But you say, wherein have we robbed thee? In tithes and offerings. Ye are cursed with a curse for ye have robbed me, even this whole nation. Bring ye all the tithes into the storehouse, that there may be meat in mine house and prove me now herewith saith the Lord of host, if I will not open the windows of heaven, and pour you out a blessing, that there shall not be room enough to receive it.* (Mal. 3:8-10)

- E. Offering has always been considered as a vital part of the adult service, but teachers often skip over it in children's service, leaving the impression that offerings are unimportant.

- F. Teach the children to give because God tells us to give and because we love God.

- G. Children need to be taught to give and to tithe, so that they can successfully become all that God intends for them to be and live in the fullness of His blessings. *Give and it shall be given unto you; good measure, pressed down and shaken together, and running over, shall men give into your bosom. For with the same measure that you mete withal it shall be measured to you again.* (Luke 6:38)

III. Encourage goodwill offering contests.

- A. Malachi 3:8-12 is the only place that God says to prove God or test him, and see the blessings he will pour out to those faithful to give.

- B. The contests are made to add excitement to the offering, but always teach children the word on giving.

- C. Contests may include a competition between the boy and girls.

- D. You can offer a reward for the children who bring the most money in a month.

- E. Divide the class into groups and have them collectively bring money. The group that wins receives an award.

F. Give the children a plastic bottle and ask friends and family to feed the bottle with change for their offering. This is how we paid for some of our playground equipment.

IV. Teach children to give because:

A. They love God.

B. They want to obey God's commandments on tithing and offerings.

C. God is always taking care of them and their needs. *But my God shall supply all your need according to his riches in glory by Christ Jesus.* (Phil. 4:19)

Worship—Entering into God's Presence

I. Worshiping God is all about our love for him.

　A. Children need to be taught how to worship.

　B. As children enter into worship, God desires to demonstrate his love in return.

　C. Worship allows children to experience God's presence.

II. Children cannot go where the teacher has not been.

　A. Teachers must spend time in worship.

　B. In preparation for the class the teacher needs to worship God.

III. Teachers and helpers can demonstrate different ways to worship by:

A. Raising their hands

B. Kneeling

C. Singing

D. Shouting

E. Dancing

F. Talking silently with God

IV. Music can help children enter into worship.

    A. Always choose music and songs that are familiar to the children.

    B. Worshiping with slow music can calm the atmosphere of the classroom.

V. God loves it when we worship Him.

    A. *Have no other gods before me.* (Deut. 5:7)

    B. God wants us to put him first and to love him.

    C. If children learn to worship God at an early age, they will always be able to hear God's voice and know it clearly.

    D. Teaching children to worship independently should be the goal of every children's minister.

VI. Worship to God

    A. Changes the children.

    B. Invites the Holy Spirit into your classroom.

    C. Allows the children to experience the presence of the Lord.

    D. Prepares the way for the Word that has been prepared to teach during that class.

    E. Brings the peace of God and the anointing of God into that class.

VII. Always put worship in your class time.

   A. *O taste and see for the Lord is good.* (Ps. 34:8) Allow the students to taste and see the Lord during worship.

   B. Be led by the Spirit of God, and be willing to change your plans if worship and prayer continue.

   C. The children will never be the same, if they experience God's presence during worship.

Object Lessons—Sermons that Connect with Kids

I. Object lessons are sermons that use visual aids to demonstrate your thought and theme.

   A. Jesus taught by demonstration.

   B. In Mark 11:12-14, Jesus used a fig tree to explain that Christians should bear fruit.

II. Object lessons can be used to demonstrate objects that can be applied to real life.

   A. A flaming Bible can be used to demonstrate that we must be hot and on fire for God, not cool or lukewarm.

   B. A road map can be used to illustrate our Christian walk with the Lord—how there is a straightway to our destination, but we can detour on different routes and get lost.

   C. Three large nails and a hammer can be used to talk about the sufferings of Jesus on the cross.

III. Ideas for an object lesson

   A. There are many places to look for ideas.

      1. The internet

        2. Christian bookstores

        3. Good Christian literature

IV.   Preparing for your object lesson

    A. Read over it a few times until you are comfortable telling it without your notes.

    B. For it to be most effective, tell your lesson from your heart.

    C. Put some prayer into your object lesson before you minister.

    D. Make sure you have all your items, to ensure that your object lesson goes smoothly.

    E. If something doesn't turn out the way you plan, keep ministering. You can admit, "This is not how I hoped this would turn out, but this is what was supposed to happen."

    F. The children do not know what was in your notes, so just be led by the Holy Spirit.

    G. Be confident in what you are saying and demonstrating.

V.   Object-lesson supplies

    A. If you have invested your money in a good object-lesson prop, be a good steward and keep it in a place where you can find it again if you need to.

    B. Designate a spot in your church for object-lesson props.

1. This spot should be in a central location so that all teachers can share it.

2. Label each container so that teachers will be able to find props easily and remember where to return items.

3. Assign a person to be in charge of prop supplies.

4. Containers in alphabetic order make items easier to find.

VI. Helpful hints

A. Do not allow the children to handle the props or objects.

B. Be creative and flexible.

C. Make sure the children know they're not magic tricks.

D. The more excited you are about what you are ministering, the more the kids will get into what you are teaching.

Puppets—A Fun Way to Minister

I. Puppets are an exciting way to minister to children.

   A. Puppets can teach God's Word in a unique way.

   B. All ages love them.

   C. Puppets are an easy way for children to express themselves.

   D. Puppets are an outlet that enables shy children to minister.

II. Helpful suggestions for puppets are:

   A. Care

   1. Be responsible in caretaking, because most puppets are expensive.

   2. Always carry the puppet by hanging the neck draped over your arm.

   B. Storage

   1. Puppets must be kept in a secure, dry place.

   2. Dowel rods or shelves can be used to store puppets safely.

C. Clothes

    1. Puppets generally wear size 24 months to 3 Toddler.

    2. Keep a variety of clothes on hand for various skits.

    3. To portray adult men, use oxford shirts, jackets, ties, etc.

    4. For Bible characters, use robes and headdresses.

    5. For women, use dresses, wigs, hats, jewelry, etc.

    6. For children, use youthful t-shirts, hair accessories, sunglasses, bandanas, etc.

III. Rods for arms:

A. Can be used to add more-lifelike actions to puppet skits.

B. Can be used to exaggerate expression.

IV. Types of puppets are:

A. People

B. Animals

C. Objects (candle, brain, heart, etc.)

D. Puppets with non-moveable mouths are great for younger children.

V. Basic rules when using puppets are:

A. Always lower the bottom jaw when talking, not the head.

B. Walk on stage as if climbing up stairs. Never jump up or just suddenly appear.

C. Exit the same way as entering—as if walking down stairs.

D. The correct puppet height is to align the belly button of the puppet to the top of the stage.

E. Synchronize opening and closing of the puppet's mouth with each syllable of the words.

F. Have the head appear to look around and move some, to make the puppet look alive.

G. The head should be held to look at the audience as if making eye contact.

VI. Puppets can be used in the ministry by:

A. Talking to the teacher during memory verse, ice-breaker, rules, etc.

B. Using pre-recorded puppet CDs.

C. Singing with music and playing musical instruments.

VII. Puppet stages can be:

A. As simple as fabric stretched between two adults.

B. Made from PVC pipe and fabric.

C. Made by turning a large table over.

D. Designed as a wooden stage on wheels.

E. Built to match the theme of the classroom.

F. Created from a very large decorated box.

G. A blanket wrapped around the puppeteer's arm works for younger children.

VIII. Voice changes can be accomplished by using:

A. A high pitch for a little boy.

B. A low voice for a man.

C. Heavy breathing when excited.

D. Slow, soft words for the heart puppet.

E. A whiney voice for a little girl.

F. Technical words when using the brain puppet.

G. Deep cynical voice for the Devil or evil characters.

H. A soft voice for a woman or mother.

IX. Practice, practice, and more practice with puppets.

A. Build muscles by holding your arm up.

B. Practice with TV commercials.

C. Practice with music, by moving and singing to the song.

Powerful Sermons and Anointed Altar Calls

I. Powerful sermons

A. Pray.

B. Be prepared. Speak from your heart, not your paper. Study and allow the Holy Spirit to speak through you. *Study to show thyself approved unto God, a workman that study to show thyself approved unto God, a workman that needeth not be ashamed, rightly dividing the word of truth.* (2 Tim 2:15)

C. Make your voice appealing.

1. Speed up, slow down, or hesitate in correspondence to the emotions, mood, or points to be conveyed.

2. Lower and raise voice appropriately. A whisper can draw attention as much as a shout.

3. Use an exciting voice, not a monotone one. Your audience will never be more excited or interested than you are.

4. Emphasize the main point. Bring focus to the biblical truth being taught.

D. Use physical language.

   1. Move about in correspondence to the lesson.

   2. Use arms and hands to help express ideas.

E. Use facial expressions.

F. Keep eye contact.

G. Involve the audience:

   1. Ask questions with an obvious answer, letting the audience repeat phrases or words.

   2. Have them participate in a particular motion or sound effect on cue.

H. Use visual aids when possible.

   1. Flannel characters

   2. Pictures or posters

   3. Objects or props

I. Be exciting and bold. God's Word is exciting and powerful—that is reason enough to be bold. *And whatsoever ye do, do it heartily, as to the Lord, and not unto men; Knowing that of the Lord ye shall receive the reward of the inheritance: for ye serve the Lord Christ.* (Col. 3:23, 24)

J. Be sincere. God's Word should minister to you as well as to your class.

II. Anointed altar calls

A. Altar calls should relate to the class you are teaching.

1. They should correspond to the lesson being taught.
2. Altar calls should be age- and maturity-appropriate.
3. They should be something the children can relate to.

B. Salvation is a concept that even young children can understand when it is explained.

1. Children do not always react like adults. They do not have great sins to cry and repent over, so even though they are making a sincere commitment, it may be unemotional.
2. The ABCs of salvation is a simple concept that children can comprehend.

    a. A is for "Accept Jesus as Savior."

    b. B is for "Believe He is the son of God and that He paid for your sins and mistakes by dying on the cross for you. Believe He rose again and is seated next to Father God and is praying for you."

    c. C is for "Be willing to *confess* Him to be your Savior and Lord, and tell others."

3. Children can understand that salvation means Jesus died to pay for your punishment for sins. He paid for forgiveness of sins, blessings here on earth, and a home in heaven. Jesus lives in your heart once you ask him to be your Lord and Savior.

      a. 'Savior' means Jesus saved you from the punishment of your sins—like someone taking your spanking.

      b. 'Lord' means you are giving Jesus the right to be in charge of your life.

C. Altar calls can cover sickness or any other situation.

   1. If it's important to the child, it is important to God. It's all right to pray for sick pets, etc.

   2. The purpose is to teach children that God hears their prayers; that God is faithful to answer those prayers; and that you can take any problem to God for he is faithful.

Storytelling—Ministry that Entertains

I. Choose a story suitable to your audience.

   A. Consider the maturity, present knowledge, and attention span of the group.

   B. Minister age-appropriately. *When I was a child, I spake as a child, I understood as a child.* (1 Cor. 13:11)

II. The story should be full of anticipation.

   A. Use exaggerations, but do not change truths in the Bible stories.

   B. Elaborate on the colorful details.

III. Know your story.

   A. Tell it in your own words.

   B. Make the story real and enjoy telling it.

   C. The love and excitement you show will shine through to the children.

IV. Use a good introduction.

   A. Hook your audience with an exciting introduction without giving away the plot or ending.

   B. Tell familiar stories with a new and exciting twist.

V. Use good narration.

    A. Enunciate your words clearly and use great expression!

    B. Use your voice to set the mood, create suspense, and express emotions such as:

        1. Happiness

        2. Sadness

        3. Excitement

        4. Anger

        5. Suspense

VI. Use details.

    A. Make sure your story comes alive.

    B. When you tell your story, make sure the children are 'seeing it' in their mind.

VII. Use good dialogue.

    A. Have the characters speak.

    B. Demonstrate conversations by changing your voice and expressions to represent the character speaking.

VIII. Pause and pace.

    A. Use speed and volume of words to draw the audience in.

    B. Slow down and speed up to correspond with the actions or moods.

        C. A whisper can be as intriguing as a shout.

IX.   Involve the audience.

        A. Have the audience repeat certain parts or do a particular motions or sound effects on cues.

        B. Ask questions with obvious answers. Jesus often asked questions to involve his audience.

X.   Use sound effects.

        A. This can be done with props.

        B. You also can imitate sounds with your voice.

        C. You can have your assistant teacher to make sound effects on cues.

XI.   Use physical language.

        A. Use eye contact.

        B. Use facial expressions.

        C. Use hand gestures.

        D. Implement movement whenever it is appropriate.

XII.   Make the application of the story strong.

        A. Build the story in suspense to a climax.

        B. Make a definite point to remember.

        C. Emphasize the theme of the lesson, pointing out examples of how the story applies to children's lives.

XIII. Be creative.

    A. Storytelling can be done in various ways:

        1. Use a variety of props, such as hats and other objects.

        2. Tell the story from a different point of view, such as a tour guide's or an animal's viewpoint, etc.

        3. Do not get into the rut of using the same techniques and props over and over.

        4. Finally, make your story a fun and exciting learning experience.

Crafts—Hands-On Projects to Teach the Word

I. Crafts can add a 'wow' factor to your sermon.

    A. Plan crafts that enhance the theme of your lesson.

    B. Crafts can also be themed for holidays.

        1. Easter crafts

        2. Christmas crafts

        3. Thanksgiving crafts

    C. Allow children to show their creative side. Don't change their work even if it is glued in the wrong spot.

    D. Each craft should be an original masterpiece.

II. Make sure the crafts are age-appropriate.

    A. If working with younger children, make sure the craft project is not too complicated.

    B. If working with older children, plan something that is more challenging.

III. Preparing a craft project

    A. There are many places to find craft ideas.

1. The internet
2. Craft books
3. Craft stores
4. Craft catalogs

B. Make sure you have enough craft projects for each child. No one should ever be left out.

C. Be sure to have made the craft ahead of time, to determine how difficult it is and how long it will take to finish. Always have enough supplies for each child, including plenty of glue, scissors, tape, etc.

D. Allow time for drying if you plan on students taking the craft home.

IV. Displaying crafts

A. Children love to see their artwork displayed.

B. Plan a spot in your church to decorate with children's work, where the masterpieces can be admired.

C. Allow children to decorate their classroom with their artwork.

D. Crafts should be fun.

E. Be creative.

V. Craft supplies

A. It is good idea to have some basic supplies on hand.

1. Glue, paint, paint brushes, tape, scissors, cotton balls, markers, ink pens, colored pencils, hot-glue gun and glue sticks, etc.

2. A good time to buy these items is in August, during back-to-school shopping.

B. Designate a spot in your church for craft supplies.

1. It should be a central location that all teachers can share.

2. Label each container so teachers will remember where to put returned items.

3. Have a message board for teachers to write down any item they may need or be running low on. For example, "Out of cotton balls" and "Need more glue sticks."

4. Assign a person to be in charge of craft supplies.

Drama—Captivating the Audience

I. Why use drama in ministry?

   A. It is an excellent way to demonstrate God's Word.

   B. Children tend to remember a skit better than just hearing a story.

   C. They get a visual, auditory, and emotional memory from a dramatic skit.

   D. It can be fun for both children and teachers.

II. Examples for using drama are:

   A. One character dresses up each week to visit the children (clowns, pink gorilla, etc.). This can be used as an ice-breaker, while making announcements, etc.

   B. Character skits using one or more characters such as a little boy talking to his little sister.

   C. Mimes perform silently or to music.

III. Hints for a successful drama are:

   A. Practice!

   B. Prepare and get everything ready, like props, costumes, and music.

- C. Use good vocal projection.
- D. Memorize the script.
- E. Continue the script, even if you mess up.
- F. Do not make eye contact with the audience.
- G. Never turn your back on the audience, unless the skit directs you to.
- H. Over-emphasize emotions.
- I. Use hand and body language to express points.
- J. Have fun with it!

IV. Ideas for dramas

- A. Design your own character, such as an old lady, a doctor, a safari adventurer, etc.
- B. Begin a clown ministry.
- C. Purchase a full-body costume such as a gorilla, a lion, a dog, etc.
- D. Write your own dramas to match the theme of the literature.
- E. Purchase drama books with skits appropriate for your drama-team audience.

Memory Verses—Creative Ways to Teach

I. God's Word is very important.

   A. The memorization of Scripture is a vital part of every believer.

   B. Memory verses should be taught in every class.

II. God's Word needs to be in our hearts and our minds.

   A. *My son, attend to my word; incline thine ear unto my sayings. Let them not depart from thine eyes; keep them in the midst of thine heart. For they are life unto those that find them and health to all their flesh."* (Prov. 4:20-22)

   B. *Let the Word of Christ dwell in you richly in all wisdom; teaching and admonishing one another in psalms and hymns and spiritual songs, singing with grace in your hearts to the Lord.* (Col. 3:16)

   C. *But the Word of our God shall stand forever.* (Isa. 40:8)

   D. *Thy Word have I hid in mine heart, that I might not sin against thee.* (Ps. 119:11)

III. God expects his children to learn and memorize his Word.

   A. *All Scripture is given by inspiration of God, and is profitable for doctrine, for reproof, for correction, for instruction in righteousness.* (2 Tim. 3:16)

IV. God's Word is our weapon against Satan's devices.

 A. *The sword of the Spirit, which is the Word of God.* (Eph. 6:17)

 B. *For the Word of God is quick and powerful and sharper than any two-edged sword.* (Heb. 4:12)

 C. Matthew 4:1-11 tells of Jesus being tempted by Satan three times. Each time, Jesus replies with the Word of God saying, "It is written."

 D. *So shall my Word be that goeth forth out of my mouth; it shall not return unto me void, but it shall accomplish that which I please, and it shall prosper in the thing whereto I send it.* (Isa. 55:11)

V. God commands us to teach the Word of God to our children.

 A. *And these words, which I command thee this day, shall be in thine heart: And thou shalt teach them diligently unto thy children, and shalt talk of them when thou sittest in thine house, and when thou walkest by the way, and when thou liest down, and when thou risest up.* (Deut. 6:6, 7)

 B. *And ye shall teach them your children, speaking of them when thou sittest in thine house, and when thou walkest by the way, when thou liest down, and when thou risest up. And thou shalt write them upon the door posts of thine house, and upon thy gates: That your days may be multiplied, and the days of your children, in the land which the Lord sware unto your fathers to give them, as the days of heaven upon the earth.* (Deut. 11:19-21)

VI. God promises blessing to those who teach the Word of God to their children.

   A. Promises long life. (Deut. 6:2)

   B. Deut. 11:19-21 promises a long life to you and to your children and days as heaven on earth.

VII. Children must know Scripture to please God, to live in victory, and to combat Satan.

   A. Simply memorizing Scripture is not effective unless the child understands and knows how to practice the use of the memory verses in his/her life.

   B. This can best be taught by tying together the lesson and memory verse with a central theme.

   C. The sermon, Bible lesson, and supplementary lessons will help bring understanding and knowledge in the use of the memory verse.

VIII. Teaching in creative and exciting ways will help them retain the knowledge of memory verses longer.

   A. The best way to teach a memory verse it to approach it as a fun activity, without discussing the memorization of the verse.

   B. Plan activities that encourage the children to repeat the verse eight to ten times as part of the fun.

   C. Repetition of a verse promotes memorization of the verse.

   D. Memory verses should be fun.

1. Puppets can be very effective.

    a. The 'silly puppet' approach brings humor and fun into the classroom. The puppeteer pretends he is trying to learn the verse and will continue to misquote it in funny ways. The children will repeat the verse, trying to rectify his mistakes in order to 'teach him' how to say the verse correctly.

    b. The 'fast-talking puppet' who brags he can say the verse faster than any of the children. One child at a time races him. The first five or more children will lose to the puppet. The other children will repeat the verse after each unsuccessful attempt, in order to help the next person or their team learn the verse, so this child can say it fast enough to win.

    c. 'Child-sized puppets' can be used for the children to say the verse. Give each child a puppet and let them change their voice to a high pitch or low pitch to say the verse.

2. Competitive games generate interest for teaching memory verses. Most any game can be modified to teach a memory verse. Simply divide the class into teams and let them compete. You can have the entire team say the verse each time. Children must say the verse to compete or get a turn. Always keep score. You can treat everyone at the end, but give the winners an extra treat.

Any game that you can think of or create can be used to teach a memory verse. Here are some of our favorite examples:

a. Squirt-Gun Duel—Two children, one from each team, stand back to back, then count off five spaces and turn to squirt each other. The first to say the memory verse wins. Then two more children duel.

b. Balloon Burst—Again, you have two teams, with one member from each team competing at a time. The two children who are competing stand side by side. The children race to see who can say the memory verse correctly. As the memory verse is completed, the child bursts a balloon. The first to burst the balloon scores.

c. Nerf Basketball—Divide the class into two teams. The children must say the memory verse to make a shot. Each successful basket scores for the team. This can be modified to work for soccer, baseball, football, hockey, golf, etc.

d. Tic Tac Toe—Large-size bean-bag toss. Divide the class into two teams. One person from one team says the verse, then they get a turn to throw the bean bag. Teams take turns saying and throwing the bean bags. Whichever team scores three in a row wins.

e. Let's Go Fishing—Put magnetic fish in a pond with points on each fish. Let the students fish with a magnetic hook after they say the memory verse for points. The team with the most points wins.

f. Velcro Dart Game—Children say the verse and get a chance to throw the dart for points.

g. Bowling—As a child says the memory verse, let him/her knock down the pins.

h. Catch the Plate—Divide into two teams, with one plate per team. Let the children carry a plastic plate on their heads to say the memory verse.

i. Relays—There are many varieties, from crab-walking to carrying spoons of jelly beans, etc.

j. Car Race—Use pocket cars and allow one member from each team to race each other after they say the memory verse. Then let the cars race to see how far or how fast the cars can go.

k. Hang the Devil—A member from each team competes saying the memory verse. The winner may draw a new piece to 'hang the Devil.'

l. Pin the Tail on the Donkey—Say the verse to get a turn at pinning the tail on the donkey.

m. Ring Toss—Make a homemade ring toss out of two-liter bottles and plastic bracelets. Let the children compete to say the verse and throw their bracelets.

n. Bean Bag Toss—Make bean bags out of old socks. Use small containers to throw bean bags into.

o. Hot Potato—You can use a Bible, ball, bean bag, or stuffed Devil, etc., to pass around a circle. When the music stops, the child holding the object must say the verse.

p. Bus Ride—Line the chairs up like bus seats. As the children say the memory verse they are allowed to get on the bus.

q. Puzzle Race—Teams race to put a puzzle together correctly to form a completed puzzle. The team who finishes first must then say the verse.

r. Red Light—One child says the verse standing with his/her back to the other children. As that child recites the verse, the other children race to get to him/her. As he/she finishes quoting the verse, he/she yells "Red Light" and turns around to see children running to him/her. Anyone seen moving has to return to the starting position. Whoever gets to him/her first says the memory verse and then gets the next turn up front.

s. Plate Twirl—Each child twirls the plate and quotes the Scripture. If he/she can quote the Scripture before the plate falls the team gets a point. Use two plates for large groups.

    t. Simon Says—As 'Simon' says to do an action the student will say the Scripture.

    u. Follow the Leader—First the teacher, then various children lead the pupils in motions while quoting the Scripture.

3. Chants and songs are fun ways to teach memory verses. Singing the Scripture or chanting it with a beat keeps the verse in the children's memory long the after service.

    a. Musical Chairs—Can be played while singing the memory verse.

    b. Freeze Frame—A ball, bean bag, or stuffed Devil can be passed until the memory verse has been quoted. The person with the object on the last word is out.

    c. Train Ride—One child begins chanting the verse while walking around the classroom. At the last word in the verse, he/she picks up another child, and they chant the verse until time to pick up more passengers. Do this until all the children are picked up.

    d. Musical Bible—Play a catchy or familiar song the children know. The children make a circle and begin to pass the Bible around the circle. When the music stops, the child holding the Bible must say the verse.

4. The written Word.

a. Living Memory Verse Line—The class is divided into two teams. Each child on both teams is given a word from the memory verse on a card. Then, the two teams of children race each other to get their memory verse words in order by standing in a straight line holding their cards where everyone can see. The first team to get in order and say the verse wins.

b. Erase the Verse—Have the verse written on a board. Erase one or more words at a time and let the class say the memory verse until all words are erased.

c. Candy Bar Game—Tape the words of the Scripture on the candy bars. Hand out the candy as each child reads the words. They race to put the verse in the right order. After doing this a few times and when the class can say the verse, they can eat the candy bars.

d. Puzzle Race—Write the words on a poster board. Then cut the board to resemble puzzle pieces. Teams race to put the words together correctly to form a completed puzzle. The team who finishes first must then say the verse.

5. Conclusion—These are just a few of the games that can be played to teach a memory verse. Be creative and invent new games in which the class can compete saying the verse before a child takes a turn.

Part III
Specialty Class Divisions

Nursery

I. Guidelines

    A. Keep the door closed at all times.

    B. Sign all children in.

    C. Receive children at the door.

    D. Only head teachers and training teachers are permitted in the nursery before, during, and after service.

        1. Only visitors are permitted in the nursery with their children, but they should be encouraged to return to service.

        2. Only when a child is distressed are parents permitted in the nursery. Once the child has calmed down, the parent should return to the service.

    E. Be sure parents are aware of how you plan to contact them if you need them. For example, assign each child a number. If the parent is needed, the number can be sent to the overhead projector to be displayed in the sanctuary. This, in turn, will alert parents to come to the nursery.

    F. Only parents, grandparents, siblings, or guardians are permitted to pick up children.

    G. Once the child has been signed in or picked up, encourage people to move so that others may have access to the door.

    H. Make sure all paperwork has been completed on all new children.

    I. Everyone working must help clean up and close down the nursery after each service.

II. Receiving the baby

    A. Welcome the baby and parents with a cheerful voice and smile.

    B. Have the parents sign the child in.

    C. Give every child a number at the time of sign-in.

    D. Explain the intention and reason for the number and where it can be found in the main sanctuary.

    E. Obtain all information, such as that needed to complete the registration sheet, when the child is signed in.

    F. Make sure all items are labeled and placed in the right cubby.

III. Ask pertinent questions.

    A. When was the last time he/she was fed?

    B. Is the child bottle or breast fed?

    C. Does your child like his/her bottle to be heated?

    D. When was the last time he or she was changed?

    E. Does the baby have a favorite toy or blanket?

    F. When will your baby need to be fed?

IV. Care

   A. If you place the babies on the floor, make sure you place a blanket down first.

   B. Always clean the bottle or pacifier if it has been dropped on the floor.

   C. Never leave a baby unattended with a bottle.

   D. Make sure you keep the baby's face, hands, and clothes clean at all times.

   E. Always handle the babies carefully and gently.

   F. Always support their head and neck with your hands.

   G. Have soft music playing at all times.

V. Illness

   A. If a baby shows signs of fever, rash, vomiting, or diarrhea, the parents should be called.

   B. If you, as a children's worker, have a fever, diarrhea, vomiting, or cold-like symptoms, please refrain from coming into contact with the babies.

VI. Dismissal

   A. Gather all of the babies' belongings.

   B. Release the baby only to the parent after he/she has signed the baby out.

   C. Tell the parent:

      1. When the baby was last changed.

      2. When the baby was fed last.

      3. How the baby did in class during service.

   D. Say good-bye.

E. Encourage all parents to bring their babies back again.

VII. Clean up

A. Everyone should participate in clean up.

B. Leave the room clean and ready for the next service.

C. Please:

1. Remove all trash and put a replacement bag back in the trash can.

2. Change sheets on the beds, if needed.

3. Disinfect all areas in the room, such as:

    a. Changing table

    b. Toys

    c. Swings

    d. Infants seats

    e. High chairs

4. Put away all ministry supplies and disinfect, if needed.

5. Close the door and turn off the lights.

Toddlers

I. Guidelines

   A. Preparation

      1. Please pray for the toddler department and its workers.

      2. Pray in the room, and speak blessings over the children.

      3. Always be on time. Arrive in class fifteen to thirty minutes early.

      4. Have all lesson materials ready before the children arrive.

      5. Be sure to have snack and drinks ready before class.

      6. Turn on soft music to help the children relax.

      7. Look around the room and make sure the room is ready for children.

   B. Receiving

      1. Each child should be greeted with kindness and love.

      2. Have the parents sign the child in.

3. Give every child a number at the time of sign-in.

4. Explain the reason for the number and where it can be found in the main sanctuary.

5. Obtain all information that is needed to complete the registration sheet, when the child is signed in.

6. Make sure all items are labeled and placed in the right cubby or coat hook.

C. During class

1. As class begins, have the children color or play to let them get familiar with the classroom environment.

2. As the children settle in, start preparing them for the lesson.

3. Have the children sit during the lesson.

4. After everyone is seated, begin teaching the lesson.

5. This can be a good time to offer some snacks. Remember 1- and 2-year-olds have very short attention spans so having snacks will help keep them seated.

D. Snack time

1. Write each child's name on a label and add it to his/her sippy-cup or bottle.

2. Show them a picture of the praying hands and explain to them what it is.

3. Say the blessing over the food.

4. Have children to bow their heads and fold their hands as you pray.

5. Keep children seated at all times during the lesson.

E. Lesson time

1. The material that is used for the lesson is used only for that purpose. Do not allow children to play with the material.

2. Here is a list of different Bible stories you can use to minister to the children.

   a. Creation

   b. Noah's ark

   c. Moses as a baby

   d. David as a shepherd boy

   e. Daniel in the lion's den

   f. The birth of Jesus

   g. Resurrection of Christ

   h. Jonah and the whale

3. Toddlers learn by repetition. Therefore the lessons are taught for at least one to two months.

F. Other ways to minister are:

1. Music.

2. Puppets.

3. Flannel board stories.

4. Crafts.

5. DVDs on the lesson that are age-appropriate.

6. Toys such as a Noah's ark with animals.

7. Picture books with Bible stories.

G. End of service

1. Change diapers that need changing.

2. Wash children's faces and hands before they leave.

3. Pick up all toys.

4. Have parents pick up children at the door, rather than allowing them to come inside.

5. Have parents sign the child out, just as they signed in.

H. Clean up

1. Begin with disinfecting the changing table and the table used during the lesson.

2. Wipe all toys with disinfectant wipes, especially those that have been put in children's mouths.

3. Vacuum the floors.

4. Wash all cups in hot soapy water.

5. Take the trash out and replace with a clean liner.

6. Turn off the light and close the door as you leave.

I. A scripture to remember is: *And whatsoever you do, do it heartily, as to the Lord and not unto men. Knowing that the Lord ye shall receive the reward of the inheritance; for ye serve the Lord Jesus Christ.* (Col. 3:23, 24)

Tips for Nursery and Toddler Teachers

I. Have a positive attitude.

　　A. Each time a baby has a pleasant experience he/she will associate that positive feeling with church.

　　B. Talk, sing and pray softly while feeding or changing a baby.

　　C. Give your full attention to the babies when you are with them.

　　D. Be sensitive to the desires of the baby.

　　E. Stimulate babies with soft music, playful songs, pages flipping in their Bible, and singing to them in the nursery.

　　F. Baby's attention spans are very short; therefore, have several items available to teach their lesson and to entertain them.

　　G. Pray and confess the Word over the babies.

II. Promote safety.

　　A. Stay alert to the babies' safety at all times.

　　B. Watch for:

1. Fingers under rocking chairs or when closing a door.

2. Broken toys.

3. Anything that can be swallowed.

C. Babies are not to be released to unauthorized people.

D. Lap and shoulder straps should be in use when a baby is in the following:

1. High chair

2. Swings

3. Infant seats

E. Crib sides should be closed at all times while a baby is in the crib.

F. Always pick babies up by placing your hands under their arms. Never pull a baby up by the arms.

III. If an accident or injury has occurred:

A. Pray.

B. Call for your coordinator.

C. Apply first-aid, if needed.

D. Inform the baby's parents.

Diaper Changing Procedures

I. Guidelines.

    A. Have all materials prepared prior to reaching for the baby.

    B. Put on disposable gloves.

    C. Never leave a baby unattended on the changing table.

    D. Cover the changing table with a disposable pad, or use the baby's own blanket or diaper pad.

    E. Lay the baby on the changing table.

    F. Remove and discard the soiled diaper.

    G. Clean the baby.

    H. Place a new diaper on the baby.

    I. Return the baby to his/her activity.

    J. Disinfect the changing table.

    K. Remove gloves by rolling one down, grabbing the other glove and putting them inside of one another to be trashed.

    L. Wash your hands before changing another baby.

Preschool Classroom Procedures

I. Be prepared.

    A. Always plan ahead.

    B. Prepare your lessons and anything you need before class starts.

    C. Class will flow more smoothly if you are prepared.

    D. Set up room for children.

        1. Put out coloring sheets and crayons.

        2. Arrange chairs and tables for ministry.

        3. Lay out flannel characters with board.

        4. Get objects ready for lesson.

        5. Get memory verse game ready to play.

        6. Select music for class.

        7. Collect anything you may need for crafts.

II. Receiving children

    A. As children enter, welcome them with a warm and loving smile.

    B. Always look the child in the eye and speak to him/her personally.

C. Remind each child how glad you are that he/she came.

D. Have parent(s) sign the child in.

E. Place child's name on belongings in his/her cubby or on his/her hook.

F. Immediately find something to catch each child's interest so they will feel accepted. Some examples include:

1. A Christian movie playing.

2. A coloring sheet.

3. Some story books.

4. Toys.

III. Praise and worship

A. At times, you may want to take the children in the main sanctuary for adult worship time.

B. Most of the time, worship should be done in class. Use upbeat songs, songs with actions to begin with, and slow songs for worship.

IV. Offering

A. Offering is a time children can learn to give to God.

B. Have a really neat container to collect the offering in.

C. Remind preschoolers that they are blessed when they give to God.

D. Allow the children to pray over the offering.

V. Review

A. Preschoolers love repetition.

B. Review often, because the children need to hear things over and over in order for them to remember. *For precept must be upon precept, precept upon precept; line upon line, line upon line; here a little, and there a little.* (Isa. 28:10)

VI. Lesson

A. Use an object or flannels to teach the lesson.

B. Never read the lesson—minister it from your heart.

VII. Memory verse

A. Preschool children cannot read; therefore you need to make sure to teach them verbally.

B. Always plan a fun game to reinforce what you are teaching.

VIII. Puppet skit

A. Animal puppets are best for preschoolers.

B. People puppets can sometimes scare this age group.

C. Never use Devil puppets in preschool.

IX. Object lesson

A. Anytime you can use an object, the child is more likely to remember what you talked about.

B. For example, when talking about David and Goliath, you could bring a real slingshot in and demonstrate how to use it.

X. Storytelling

A. Preschoolers love stories.

B. They love for you to read to them.

C. They also love when you change your voice with the characters.

D. If you tell a story, use visuals such as posters, objects, or flannel characters.

XI. Bathroom break

A. Remember that with this age group, you may need to let them visit the bathroom more frequently.

B. Take them to the bathroom as a group.

C. Make sure each child washes his/her hands.

XII. Snack time

A. Always be aware of any child who may have food allergies.

B. Try to avoid high-sugar snacks.

C. Cold water is the drink choice for preschoolers.

D. Always pray before you eat.

E. Allow one or two children to help serve the snack.

XIII. Craft time

A. Crafts can be a great way to reinforce the lesson.

B. The craft should be fun and age-appropriate.

C. Be sure to always say something to make the child feel proud of his/her artwork.

D. Make sure the child does his/her own artwork.

E. Allow for drying time and plan accordingly.

XIV. Play time

A. Sometimes services run long and extra time slots can be added, allowing the children some structured play time.

B. Only pull out certain toys and allow children to play with them for a certain amount of time. Then after about eight to ten minutes, allow them to exchange toys with other children.

XV. Dismissal

A. Allow the person who signed the child in to pick up the child.

B. Only if the parent or guardian makes other arrangements shall someone else pick up the child. Never allow just anyone to pick up the child.

C. Make sure each child takes all belongings.

D. Always hug each child, reassure him/her about how good he/she was, and tell him/her that you can't wait until next service.

XVI. Clean up

A. Make sure your room is clean, just like when you arrived.

B. Disinfect all toys, table, etc.

C. Vacuum the floor.

D. Take out the trash.

Class Procedure
Children's Church and Preteens

I. Always begin class with prayer.

    A. Take care of the physical needs of the children first. Allow them to go the bathroom and get a drink of water before class. Try to avoid bathroom breaks during the ministry time.

    B. Lead the children in praise and worship songs, either in the classroom or in the sanctuary as a group.

    C. You may serve snacks at the beginning or the end of class. Just remember that some children may not have had breakfast or dinner.

    D. Always pray over the food.

    E. Receive the offering at the beginning of class, so the children won't lose or play with their money. Always teach the importance of giving by using Scriptures, having contests, or letting children know there is a need for something.

    F. Have a scheduled service planned each time, but be flexible. Circumstances may arise at anytime, such as a child in need of immediate prayer, interruptions, or an accident that could cause you to vary from your scheduled class. You'll just be doubly prepared for the next service.

G. Follow the leading of the Holy Spirit and have an altar call accordingly.

H. Never let the children leave the classroom without permission.

I. Remember that the children are your responsibility from the time they enter into the classroom until the time they leave.

J. Always put away all your teaching materials, clean the room, and leave the classroom ready for next class.

Example of a Class
Preschool, Children, and Preteens

Here is a suggested order of class. Be flexible and try not to do the same thing all the time. Constantly add new things and change the order of events to keep the children interested.

This schedule is a basic outline. Each lesson can differ, so you may need to adjust it.

Please keep in mind that the attention span of children is approximately one minute per year of age.

_____Prayer

> 1. Have intercessory prayer for the first five minutes of class.
>
> 2. Choose someone from a prayer team, the children's pastor, another teacher, or even you to lead the children in prayer.

_____Praise and Worship

> 1. Choose to do in the class or in the sanctuary with adult praise and worship.
>
> 2. Be prepared for salvation. For example, have a brochure explaining salvation ready to give to those who are saved.

_____Puppet Skits

    1. Get your older puppet team to come and do skits for you.

    2. The teacher should have prepared the skits, and the puppets should be in place.

_____Receive the Offering

    1. Choose a child to pray and receive the offering.

    2. Have one of the children count and put away the offering.

_____Announcements

    1. Go over classroom rules.

    2. Explain about quiet seat rules and rewards.

    3. Go over any field trips or church functions that include the children.

_____Memory Verse Game

    1. Choose a game the children will enjoy.

    2. Always keep the number of kids you have playing in mind when choosing a game.

_____Worship Song

    1. Slow the pace of the class down.

    2. Choose something children are familiar with.

    3. Get your children ready to receive the Word.

_____Lesson Introduction

    1. Review from previous lessons.

    2. Begin to tell what the theme is going to be about.

_____Object Lesson

    1. Have materials ready.

    2. Be sure to have practiced at home before you try it at church.

_____Bible Story

    1. Find your flannel characters and have your flannel board or visuals ready.

    2. Have props ready.

_____Drama Skit

    1. Have costumes and props ready.

_____Sermon and Altar Call

    1. Always make an altar call.

    2. Be prepared—for salvation, for example, have a brochure ready to give it them about salvation.

    3. Be sure to make sermons and altar calls age-appropriate in content and length.

_____Review with Questions

    1. Ask the children questions to find out if they were listening.

_____Snacks

> 1. Have snacks ready prior to class.
>
> 2. Never leave class alone to run and get a snack.

_____Announce Quiet Seat Prize

> 1. Give out prizes like candy or small trinket toys for the children who answer the questions correctly.
>
> 2. Reward good behavior.

_____Dismissal

> 1. Make sure each child is picked up by an adult parent.
>
> 2. Make sure they get all their belongings.

Schedule for Sunday Morning Class   Date:_____

Teacher and/or Aide	Time	Ministry
	10:00-10:30	Set Up Class and Welcome Children
	10:30-10:40	Prayer
	10:40-11:00	Praise and Worship
	11:00-11:10	Puppet Skits
	11:10-11:15	Offering
	11:15-11:20	Announcements
	11:20-11:40	Memory Verse Game
	11:40-11:45	Worship
	11:45-11:50	Lesson Introduction
	11:50-11:55	Object Lesson
	11:55-12:05	Bible Story
	12:05-12:15	Drama Skit
	12:15-12:20	Sermon and Altar Service
	12:20-12:25	Review and Questions
	12:25-12:30	Snacks
	12:30-12:40	Clean up

Schedule for Sunday Evening Class   Date:_____

Teacher and/or Aide	Time	Ministry
	6:00–6:30	Set Up Class and Welcome Children
	6:30–6:40	Prayer
	6:40–7:00	Praise and Worship
	7:00–7:10	Puppet Skits
	7:10–7:15	Offering
	7:15–7:20	Announcements
	7:20–7:40	Memory Verse Game
	7:40–7:45	Worship
	7:45–7:50	Lesson Introduction
	7:50–7:55	Object Lesson
	7:55–8:05	Bible Story
	8:05–8:15	Drama Skit
	8:15–8:20	Sermon and Altar Service
	8:20–8:25	Review and Questions
	8:25–8:30	Snacks
	8:30–8:40	Clean up

Schedule for Wednesday Evening Class   Date:_____

Teacher and/or Aide	Time	Ministry
	6:30–7:00	Set Up Class and Welcome Children
	7:00–7:10	Prayer
	7:10–7:30	Praise and Worship
	7:30–7:40	Puppet Skits
	7:40–7:45	Offering
	7:45–7:50	Announcements
	7:50–8:00	Memory Verse Game
	8:00–8:05	Worship
	8:05–8:10	Lesson Introduction
	8:10–8:15	Object Lesson
	8:15–8:25	Bible Story
	8:25–8:35	Drama Skit
	8:35–8:40	Sermon and Altar Service
	8:40–8:45	Review and Questions
	8:45–9:00	Snacks
	9:00–9:10	Clean up

Part IV
Preparing Children for Ministry

....

Encouraging Children to Minister

I. Children:

    A. Are assets in the body of Christ.

    B. Can do most anything an adult can.

    C. Need to be trained.

    D. Love to minister.

    E. Are not prideful or ashamed.

    F. Are always willing to do 'whatever' even on a short notice.

II. Ministry opportunities for children can include:

    A. Puppet team.

    B. Drama team.

    C. Dance team.

    D. Children's choir.

III. Practice is essential.

A. Choose a time devoted to practice at least once a week.

B. Always begin practice with prayer.

C. If you do all four teams, you may consider spending fifteen to twenty minutes with each team.

D. When teaching something new, the instructor should always demonstrate the first time.

E. Record a video of each puppet song, dance, drama, and choir, so you can remember exactly how you performed it and want it performed. Also, children love to watch videos of themselves.

F. Never practice with an original CD. Always make a copy just in case it gets scratched or misplaced.

G. Plan for upcoming events, and practice with each team until you feel they have the piece perfected.

Training Children to Use Puppets in Ministry

I. Training

   A. Age and size of children must be the first consideration.

   B. This will determine the types of puppets to purchase or make.

II. Preschool, kindergarten, and first-grade children

   A. This age works better with the smaller animal or people puppets without a mouth.

   B. These children may be taught to move the puppets rhythmically or to make them sway from side to side in time with the music.

   C. They may be taught to nod the head and move with nods, etc. when another character is talking or singing.

   D. Prerecorded skits or music are the easiest and best for this age group.

   E. Always choose short skits and songs, since their arms become tired quickly.

III. Children grades two through five

   A. This age group needs medium- to small-size puppets with mouths.

   B. These children have the ability to start synchronizing the mouth with the words.

   C. They are able to move in beat to the music in short- to medium-length songs.

IV. Children grades six through eight

   A. They are able to use large human puppets with wide mouths.

   B. They can perform an average-length skit or song lasting approximately five to seven minutes with practice and training.

   C. They are generally able to synchronize the mouth movements of the puppets with life-like movements and to synchronize dance movements to the rhythm of a song.

   D. They make excellent class puppet assistants to the adult teachers when they have been correctly trained in the use of puppets.

V. Training puppeteers

   A. Begin with the basics and add difficult movements and scripts as the puppeteers are ready.

   B. Begin using hands only (no puppets) to help with hand and arm positions.

VI. Basic movements

A. Entrances and exits

   1. To enter, a puppeteer should stretch the puppet behind him/her and then walk to position by using a slight bounce to directly above the puppeteer's heads. This should take three to five bounces.

   2. To exit, the puppeteer should turn the puppets head to face behind the puppeteer's head and then bounce from the position above the puppeteer's head to the shoulder, as though the puppeteer and the puppet were embracing.

   3. These bouncing movements give the puppet the appearance of climbing stairs to enter and of descending stairs to exit. This prevents the puppet from popping on stage and then appearing to drop off the stage.

B. Arm position

   1. The puppeteer's arms should be held above the head at a very slight angle to the front.

   2. This helps to prevent tiredness and allows use of the other arm for supporting the puppet-holding arm when needed.

   3. It also positions the puppet correctly for the audience.

C. Puppet position

   1. The puppet's belly button should be level with the height of the stage.

   2. Lower than that makes it hard to see the

puppet, whereas higher than that may expose the puppeteer's arm.

D. Head position

1. The head of the puppet should move in slight, graceful movement, as though it's looking around. Any puppet completely still will not be life-like but will appear artificial.

2. Limp puppets appear dead.

3. Be sure to practice life-like movements.

E. Puppet eyes

1. Puppet eyes should be looking at the audience most of the time.

2. Puppets should never look at the ceiling nor the floor, unless it is a part of the skit.

3. The correct position is done by holding four fingers in the mouth of the puppet pointing straight out and parallel to the floor.

4. The thumb will be in the chin.

5. Once the five basics are mastered, more difficult movements may be added.

F. Dance movements

1. May be added, beginning with the basics of swaying or bouncing from side to side according to the music. Add more difficult moves as the team becomes experienced.

G. Mouth synchronization

1. This is moving the mouth realistically to the words that the puppet is singing or dancing.

2. Basic rules

   a. Place four fingers in the upper head and the thumb in the chin. To talk, drop the thumb. Do not move the upper fingers or the head will appear to flop. As people drop their chin to talk, so should the puppet.

   b. The thumb or chin of the puppet should drop on each syllable. Most school children know how to clap on syllables, so to drop the thumb in synchronization to the syllables is not a hard concept for them to learn.

H. Learning voices

1. Learning voices is a more difficult concept and should only be introduced to older puppeteers who are better readers.

2. Younger children are better with CDs because they are non-readers or are slow and unsure in their reading skills, making it difficult to add voices. New puppeteers also struggle to do movements and mouth synchronization.

I. Practices

1. Puppeteers should practice once a week, starting a new song or skit at least two months in advance for special performances, such as a Christmas program, etc.

2. Begin all new skits, songs, or concepts without puppets and then add them after a little practice.

J. Ministry

1. Children's puppet teams can be very successful.

2. These puppeteers can be an asset to the children's ministry in the church and allow opportunities for these children to minister outside the church in an exciting and unique way. As always, be sure to help all the puppeteers and trainers to realize it is a ministry and not a performance. Pray together at each practice and before each ministry opportunity. Let God's love and anointing use the puppets to touch the lives of others.

Developing a Drama Team

I. The drama team will depend on the age and number of children that are available in your church.

    A. Drama teams can be developed with children ages 4 through 12 years in a children's ministry.

    B. Due to their limited reading skills, children in preschool through second grade are best used in pantomimes or in skits with very few lines.

    C. Pupils in grades three through seven are better at the spoken scripts.

    D. Begin a team with whatever age groups you have, and then separate the groups as you grow in number.

II. The basic qualifications for joining the drama could be:

    A. Must be faithful to attend rehearsals.

    B. Must be willing to study and prepare.

III. Have children and parents sign a permission slip, with the qualifications attached.

IV. Schedule practices to accommodate busy schedules.

    A. Have practice at least once a week.

B. Usually scheduling an hour before a mid-week service saves the parents an extra trip.

C. Pray, and choose a time that will be most convenient, to prevent absenteeism.

D. Allow several weeks to learn most skits.

E. Allow more time for difficult skits for special presentations, such as Easter.

V. Choosing appropriate skits will encourage success. Choose skits based on:

A. Theme

B. Length

C. Difficulty

D. Age of the pupils

E. Ability to adapt them to the team

1. Adapt your skits to fit the age and number of children.

2. You can write in extra parts.

3. You can divide one character's lines between two characters, if doing so doesn't alter the meaning, comprehension and the flow of the skit.

4. You can write your own skits to meet the needs of your group.

VI. Basic rules.

A. Speak loudly.

B. Speak clearly.

C. Stay in character, even if you make a mistake. Continue on in character until you are completely out of the scene. Remember, no one in the audience has read the script to realize there was a error.

D. Face the audience.

E. Do not make eye contact with audience.

F. Be aware of stage position. Do not fall off the stage or trip over objects.

G. Avoid unnecessary movement or whispering.

H. Be natural, not mechanical.

I. Over-emphasize emotions.

J. Use hands and body language to express points.

K. Review rules quickly at each practice.

   1. Children need to be reminded of rules more frequently than do adults.

   2. Explain the rules in simple terms.

   3. Demonstrate the rules and the reasons for them.

VII. Assign parts based on:

A. Voice

B. Character

C. Ability

D. Age

E. Allow everyone a chance to have a part in the skits you are practicing.

VIII. Demonstrate.

    A. An explanation alone will not be as effective as a demonstration of the points.

        1. The tone of your voice

        2. Dramatic changes in your voice

        3. Dramatic body language

        4. Dramatic emotions

        5. Stage positions, such as the directions to face

        6. Voice projection

IX. Keep records. Create a folder for each child.

    A. Make a copy of each skit the child is in and highlight the child's part.

    B. Require children to bring the skit folder to each practice.

    C. The director should have a folder on each drama. The folder should contain the following:

        1. An original copy of each drama

        2. Character assignments; label this information on the front of the folder.

        3. Extra copies

        4. Stage directions

        5. Places and dates of performance to prevent repetition. Remember, in the beginning, this is easy to remember, but as the team grows and performs more frequently, this book-keeping can help you plan your events more easily.

X.   Prayer and preparation are necessary.

    A. This will prevent poor performance.

    B. Drama is entertaining; many in the audience will let down their guard and forget it is ministry.

    C. Be sure that young actors and directors never forget the reason for drama is to continue to spread the Gospel of Jesus Christ.

    D. Hearts can be touched and lives changed through a simple skit. It is indeed a ministry and must be treated as such.

Dancing with a Purpose

I. Why use dance in children's ministry?

    A. Children's ministry can effectively use dance as a method of worship.

    B. Children have a heart to worship God. They are not afraid to express themselves in worship.

    C. Children need to be taught how to worship God in sign language and expressive heartfelt motions that bring glory to Him.

    D. People were created to worship God.

II. They are scriptural reasons for dance.

    A. *To everything there is a season, and a time to every purpose under the heaven.* (Eccl. 3:1)
A time to weep, a time to laugh, a time to mourn and a time to dance. (Eccl. 3:4)

    B. *And David and all the house of Israel played before the Lord on all manner instruments. David danced before the Lord with all his might. David and all the Israelites shouted with joy.* (2 Sam 6:5, 14, 15)

    C. When you are freed from sadness, dance.
Thou hast turned for me my mourning into dancing. (Ps. 30:11, 12)

D. When you are saved or freed from bondage, dance. *Then Aaron's sister Miriam, who was a prophetess, took a tambourine n her hand. All the women followed her, playing tambourines and dancing.* (Ex. 15:20)

E. When you are in church service, dance. *The daughters of Shiloh came out to dance during the feast of the Lord that was celebrated each year.* (Jud. 21:21)

F. When you have won the victory, dance. *[David] is the man the Israelite women sing about when they dance. They celebrated David's victories in battle.* (1 Sam. 21:11)

G. *Then young women of Israel will be happy and dance. The young men and old men will also dance in anticipation of the Lord's return.* (Jud. 21:19-23)

H. Dance just for fun. *Go forth in dances of them that make merry.* (Jer. 31:4)

I. There was music and dancing to celebrate the prodigal son's homecoming. (Luke 15:25)

J. Dancing in the Spirit is an impulsive outburst of joyous feeling that cannot find sufficient expression in voice or in gesture alone.

III. The mission for the Children's Dance Team is to encourage children to have a stronger relationship with the Lord.

A. Worship the Lord.

1. If we worship in practice and at home, worship will be greater, more intense, and more sincere.

2. The anointing will increase when ministering in service, when it comes from a life of worship.

B. Pray!

1. The children are encouraged to pray.

2. Emphasis is put on the importance of praying at home.

3. The dance team should always pray before practice.

C. Read the Bible.

1. Research to see what the Bible has to say about worship.

2. Teach the children Scriptures on dance so they understand that it is a form of worship.

D. Develop unity.

1. Pray for unity among the dance team.

2. As children worship the Lord together, they can experience the love of God has for them.

E. Dance should never be a show but a ministry.

F. Dance should be a form of worship not entertainment.

IV. Some tips when working with dance are:

A. Set a time for practice.

B. Before teaching the children a dance, all adults helping should learn the songs prior to practice.

C. Make sure all adults are working with all the children.

D. Boys and girls both should dance. For example, David was called a man after Gods' own heart. He stood, bowed, prostrated, raised his hands, led a procession, leaped, and twirled before everyone.

E. Teach children to submit to and respect authority.

F. Purchase or make dance costumes.

G. Pray diligently for this ministry.

H. Be committed, dedicated, and devoted.

Singing for the Lord

I. Starting a children's choir

    A. Talk with the children's pastors for permission and insight regarding how they feel about having a choir and their goals for it.

    B. Write down your vision and goals.

    C. Before starting, make sure you are committed and that you are willing to dedicate the time, effort, and prayer needed to make it the best it can be.

II. Resources for songs

    A. Christian bookstores

    B. Music stores

    C. Internet

    D. Radio

III. Recruiting

    A. Make an announcement in the church.

    B. Put it in your church bulletin.

    C. Have your teachers announce it in class.

IV. Learning a song

    A. Listen to the song for several days to make sure it is the one God wants.

    B. Introduce the song to the children and make copies for every child before practice. This will speed up the initial practice.

    C. If the song has hand motions or sign language, go over it slowly after the children have learned the song.

    D. Devote the whole practice time to one song.

    E. Pray about choosing the right child to sing any solo parts.

    F. Ask God to direct you in choosing the children for each part and for the anointing.

V. Keeping the children interested

    A. If you choose the right song, the anointing is there, and the children truly will respond.

    B. Be sure to praise the children after each performance.

About the Authors

Sharon Wicker

Sharon Wicker holds a Bachelor of Arts in Nursery-Preschool and Elementary Education and has taught in the public school system for thirty-six years. She and her husband Rod are the Pastors at Word of Victory Fellowship in Elk Garden, Virginia. Sharon has been involved with children's ministry for thirty-five years, during which she has experienced the power of God in children's lives. Sharon and Rod are blessed to have two wonderful sons, Heath (and wife Amanda) and Evan (and wife Philisha), and two grandsons, Aden and Ian, who add pleasure to their days.

Rebecca Cook

Using her degree in Early Childhood and her Bachelor of Arts in Elementary Education, Rebecca Cook has taught in public schools for fourteen years. In addition, she and her husband, Mark, are Children's Directors-Pastors at Word of Victory Fellowship, Elk Garden, Virginia. Rebecca has witnessed God pour his spirit on the children during the twenty-five years she has served in children's ministry. Rebecca and Mark love to travel, especially to see their only daughter, Stephanie (and husband Cody), in Victoria, Texas.

www.ingramcontent.com/pod-product-compliance
Lightning Source LLC
Chambersburg PA
CBHW070641050426
42451CB00008B/251